BRITISH RAILWAY
COACHING STOCK IN COL
For the Modeller and Historian

Robert Hendry

MIDLAND
An imprint of
Ian Allan Publishing

CONTENTS

First published in 2002
Reprinted 2008

ISBN 978 1 85780 145 3

Published by Midland Publishing
an imprint of Ian Allan Publishing Ltd.

Printed in England by
Ian Allan Printing Ltd.,
Hersham, Surrey, KT12 4RG

Code: 0810/A

Visit the Ian Allan Publishing website at:
www.ianallanpublishing.com

Title Page: Arguably the most important coaching stock design of all time, the British Railways Mark I was not a single vehicle type, but a range of stock covering passenger carriages, parcels vans, utility vans, post office vans and even horseboxes. Development of a range of standard carriages was an early priority of the Railway Executive in 1948. Despite serious post-war arrears of maintenance and shortages of material, and the need to blend the best from the LMS, LNER, GWR and Southern, the prototype coaches were built as early as September 1950. Production carriages appeared the following year. It was a world of rationing carried over from a war that had been over for just five years. Queen Elizabeth II had yet to ascend the throne, Britain still ruled an Empire, and TV was unknown to all but a privileged few. The world has changed dramatically since the Mk I first appeared, yet half a century after it first entered service, Mk Is can still be found in traffic on the privatised rail network. W13074 was one of twelve Corridor Firsts or FKs, built to Diagram116 at Swindon in 1953 under Lot 30066. Allocated to the Western Region from new, it was one of the coaches selected to receive the re-born GWR colours from 1956 onwards, and one of the few Mk Is to be equipped with Swindon designed B4 bogies before the regional colours were suppressed in the mid-sixties. W13074 is seen at Leamington Spa on 3rd July 1964.

Front cover top: Sometimes a photographer can strike lucky with a rare vehicle in ideal weather conditions. When I photographed M255M running north through Rugby on a stock train ex Wolverton in July 1964, I realised I had found something very exciting, but it was a long time before I realised just how lucky I had been. It had been built as one of the original batch of LMS third class sleepers in 1928, and rebuilt after the war as a Cafeteria car. To combine a rare class to begin with, an unusual rebuild mixing different styles of design, and its location as the last vehicle on the train giving a rare chance to study an LMS gangway was too good an opportunity to miss. The last of the class had gone within 18 months.

Front cover lower : If this view had been taken of a 'King Arthur' on a modern railtour, it would rank as a good shot in its own right, but it was taken more than sixty years ago, and is one of the few really outstanding pre-war action shots of a Southern Railway express train at speed. With film speeds as slow as 6-10 ASA, compared to the 200 to 400 ASA of modern film, it is a remarkable photographic achievement. It depicts No 772 *Sir Percivale*, a Maunsell "King Arthur" class 4-6-0, approaching Hewish Summit, west of Crewkerne at about midday, with what is thought to be the 8.45am ex Waterloo, on Saturday 13th August 1938. The leading coaches are also of Maunsell design, the first two carriages being diagram 2005 open thirds. The view epitomises a Southern Railway express in the last few months before the dark clouds of war dimmed the glories of the Big Four companies forever. Looking at it, I can imagine the warmth of a summer day, the trill of bird song in the trees, and the beat of an engine working hard. I can imagine crowds of happy holidaymakers, the children particularly excited that their journey to the West Country is almost over, looking keenly out of the windows of the carriages. Maybe you were one of those children, or perhaps your father or grandfather had such memories.

Above: Most enthusiasts will know of the Rainhill Trials in 1829, when different steam locomotives were pitted against one another in a competition to decide the best design. George and Robert Stephenson's *Rocket* won the competition and gained immortality, whilst one of its competitors, Timothy Hackworth's *Sanspareil* also survived into preservation. Seeing these locomotives on static display is one thing, but one of the pleasures of the last quarter of the twentieth century has been the appearance of several replica locomotives and carriages, including *Sanspareil*. As a result, we can relive travel at the dawn of the railway age. For the lower orders, open four-wheel carriages sufficed. They were derived from the traditional farm cart, and were devoid of bodywork above waist height. In 1844 Parliament, moved by the plight of third class passengers, compelled the railway companies to provide at least one Third class train with covered stock, on every line, every day. The replica train is seen at Pickering on the North Yorkshire Moors Railway in 2000.

INTRODUCTION

In the Introduction to British Railway Signalling in Colour, I recorded that the starting point for that book had been shopping trips to Leamington Spa. Whilst my father and I were waiting for my mother in the car, he taught me the block code, which I had mastered long before such boring things as the multiplication tables. The foundations for this book were laid at the same time. Some of my earliest recollections of coaching stock are of carmine and cream Mk Is at Leamington Spa, and it has been a pleasure to include such a rake in this book. Criticised at the time, many people now regard it as one of the most eye-catching coaching stock liveries ever, and the sundry liveries of the past 50 years have been a poor attempts to compete with it.

My parents had family roots in the Isle of Man, and the railways of the island were another early interest, with coaches in an equally vivid red and cream livery. In the 1950s, when there was little published on the railway, my father realised that its' largely Victorian carriage fleet was of great historic importance, and set out to photograph every coach. He actually achieved this, though one coach was broken up just after he filmed it, and the post office lost the film! Using photographs, notes and dimensions, he created a register of building dates, makers and designs.

Visits to the Isle of Wight revealed another vintage carriage fleet. In that instance our interest had been stimulated in a series of articles by Geoffrey Kichenside in the Model Railway Constructor. He was also the author of one of the first important books on coaching stock. Trips to Northern Ireland introduced us to the Ulster Transport Authority, and vehicles that ranged from 1890s bogies to steel bodied designs that would still look modern today. Through the generous help of J H Houston, Chief Mechanical Engineer of the UTA, we received a selection of rolling stock lists and drawings.

These early trips were with my father, but my first individual photographic 'scoop' came in 1964 when my father was visiting patients as a general practitioner, and I went 'Duchess' hunting at Rugby station in the last weeks of steam on the West Coast Main Line. A down stock train came through from Wolverton, with several vehicles in ex works condition . This was just before the introduction of the XP64 livery and the corporate image, so they must have been some of the last vehicles finished in coaching stock maroon. I was able to photograph a number of vehicles in the train.

The 1950s and 1960s were the Mark I era on BR, and we recorded what seemed to be a wide selection, maybe even an excessive quantity, of these highly standardised vehicles. Later I discovered just how varied the Mk I range was, and wished we had filmed more! Pre-nationalisation coaches were still around and Hawksworth, Gresley, Stanier or Bulleid stock was a welcome change to the Mk I. Elderly vehicles were still to be found. I recall the excitement when we discovered not one, but two different pre-grouping carriages at Stamford station. One was a Great

Central 'Barnum', the other an ex Great Northern Railway 6-wheeler. As a child, I saw the elegant Pullman cars on the *Bournemouth Belle*, and read that the first Pullman cars to run in England were imported from the United States for the Midland Railway in the 1870s. I never expected to see one, but by chance we found the grounded body of an American Pullman car. Years later, I found out that it was much rarer than I had first thought, for it was not a Midland example of which several survived, but the *Iona* of the Great Northern Railway.

We collected material about coaching stock, and discovered the massive contribution of the big rolling stock manufacturers. Many enthusiasts could list locomotive works, such as Crewe, Swindon or Derby, and will be familiar with builders such as Robert Stephenson, Beyer Peacock or the North British Locomotive Company. Some towns, such as Manchester, Leeds and Glasgow became celebrated locomotive building centres. Birmingham is not a name that most enthusiasts associate with railway manufacturing, but the West Midlands was a major force in the railway supply industry, the emphasis being on coaching stock. Companies such as J Wright, Brown Marshalls, Metropolitan Railway Carriage & Wagon and Oldbury all had large works in the area, and produced coaches for the small companies, for many of the bigger companies and for the legion of overseas railways that came to Britain for equipment. I found a magnificent 1850s coloured portrait of a royal coach sent from Birmingham to Egypt. As I looked at it, I realised it told me a great deal about contemporary British stock of the 1850s, for which there appear to be few if any contemporary coloured views.

Most coaching stock books examine a particular company or period. This permits an in-depth focus, but precludes a broader approach, where we can see how the stage coach of pre-railway days, the Birmingham-built Khedival coach of the 1850s, the Festiniog bogie stock of the 1870s, the Isle of Wight stock of the 1900s, the 1930s Manchester, South Junction & Altrincham electric sets or BR Diesel Multiple Units share a common ancestry. Whilst it may seem that the latest Pendolino tilting trains bear little relationship to the stagecoach, the link is there, for the modern loading gauge is effectively the loading gauge of the 1830s. That was the result of practical experience, and contrary to popular belief, was not determined by motive power needs, but by the height that was necessary to permit the pioneer railwaymen to load a gentleman's private horse drawn carriage onto an open carriage truck. Unlike America or Russia, where road bridges were rare, and a 16-foot loading gauge emerged, the British gauge was more constricted. Without rebuilding every bridge in the land, it will remain so. The Sprinters, Pacers and Turbos of today, even the Virgin Pendolinos that are being delivered as this book went to press, are all influenced by the size of horse-drawn coaches that existed before Queen Victoria came to the throne in 1837. I cannot vouch for this story, but I recall being told that the design of the private carriage of early 19th century Britain was influenced by the height of the then fashionable top hat, for it was deemed essential that a gentleman should be

able to sit in his carriage, wearing his high hat. If this is true, it may be that the outline of Sir Richard Branson's Pendolino owes much to the hatters of 200 years ago! Perhaps we owe our forbears another debt, for our average height is significantly greater than in those days. Had it not been for our forbears taste in hats, our modern carriages might be much less suited to the taller traveller of today!

In considering how to present coaching stock in colour, I had to consider the scope of the book, for one of the paradoxes of railways is that neat definitions always break down. A BR Mark 1 is a coach. A Gresley A4 is a locomotive, but what is a steam railcar, or a DMU? They are self-propelled, which is a characteristic of a locomotive, but carry passengers, which makes them coaching stock. I decided that steam railcars, DMUs and Electric Multiple Units do count. A First or 1st/3rd Composite carriage counts, as would a Brake 3rd, but if passenger carrying was the sole criteria, a full brake would not count. A full brake which ran in the same trains as passenger carrying stock had to be built to the same standards, and the railways applied the term 'NPCV' or 'NPCC' to such non passenger carrying coaching stock vehicles for this reason. Some vehicles, such as a full brake must qualify, but as soon as the NPCV is admitted, the floodgates open to a plethora of stock.

In the early days of railways, the gentry often took their private carriages with them when they travelled, so carriage trucks for use on passenger trains evolved. As they ran at passenger train speeds, the railway companies classed them as coaching stock. Farm carts were similar in size to a gentleman's carriage, and required a similar wagon when they were moved by rail. However they went by goods trains and so counted as freight stock. The gentry might take their horses with them, to haul their carriage or for hunting, so horse boxes evolved, and were classed as passenger stock. Farmers sent cows to market, but they were usually conveyed in freight trains, so were goods stock, but for very valuable cattle, the prize cattle van was developed. This looked like a horsebox, and sometimes horseboxes were used for prize cattle, and vice versa. Predictably the prize cattle van was coaching stock.

In the early days, most freight was moved in open 4 wheel wagons, but the need to keep some goods dry led to the covered goods van. The covered van was classified as freight stock, but fish, meat or fruit might perish if run on slow goods trains. Most railways built special vans for such traffic, some classing them as wagons, as they looked far more like wagons than carriages. Others classed them as coaching stock, as they ran in passenger trains, or at higher speeds. Opinions differed as to what was a coach and what was a wagon, and ideas changed over the years. A vehicle could start life as a wagon and become a carriage or vice versa. I would like to lay down clear rules, but railwaymen themselves differed. The main guidelines were appearance, construction and usage, but in differing proportions, depending on who was involved. This is the rule-of-thumb I have followed. If it looks like a coach, has coaching stock characteristics, or was commonly used on passenger or fast parcels or perishable trains, it is eligible for this volume. The cynic might say that such a definition equals what I want it to mean. He would be correct, that is how railwaymen interpreted it. At some stage in the history of railways, I am sure that an experienced railwayman instructing a junior employee must have said something along the lines of, 'this carriage is really a wagon, but that wagon is actually a carriage'.

In developing this book, a broadly chronological approach seemed preferable, as it permits the reader to see how coaching stock evolved from the 1830s. However some themes are better treated in a single section, including constructional features that are seldom seen by the enthusiast. As a modeller, I know how some details can be hard to work out. Front three quarter photos of engines are plentiful, but photos of the top of the tender are rare. A selection of views looks at 4 and 6 wheel coach underframes and what a BR Mk I looks like from underneath. The role of the commercial carriage builders, such as Metropolitan Railway Carriage & Wagon Co, Oldbury, Brown Marshalls & Co is also best highlighted in one section.

The subject is so vast that omission is inevitable. If your favourite company is not covered, I may have agonised over omitting the view you would have liked to see, but something else took priority. In other cases, there may not be any colour pictures available. Until the 1970s, works photos tended to be monochrome, and most enthusiasts, if they recorded coaching stock at all, followed suit. Colour photography was a minority interest, and in taking such photos of carriages in the 1950s or 1960s, my father was in a minority within a minority. I am very grateful for the record he started, but information on carriages, wagons or signalling was very limited. On a photographic trip, you used finite filming resources and time on what seemed to be rare or unusual. We must have seen and ignored important vehicles that deserved recording in colour without realising it. I only wish that we could have had the cameras and high-speed films of today when so many exciting vehicles were still around.

To understand the British coach of today, let alone the classic vehicles of the 1900s, you must go back to the dawn of the passenger carriage, so the starting point for this book was simple. The point at which to finish was not so easy. At first, I planned to cover designs introduced up to the end of the BR steam in 1968, which would make this volume identical with the first volume on wagons in this series. As I gathered material, I realised that so many important designs appeared between 1960 and 1968 that if I went that far, justice could not be done to them and earlier designs. I decided to cover designs introduced from the 1830s and up to 1960. Even then there is much that never made it to the finished book. The wagon story will be continued in a companion volume under preparation, and hopefully we will look at the shape of passenger stock from 1960 to 2000 in a future volume.

As with the wagon and signalling volumes in this series, I have ranged further than British Railways and its constituents. It was on the narrow gauge in Wales and the Isle of Man that some of the first bogie carriages in the British Isles appeared. Some of the first successful diesel railcars ran in Ireland. There, the Ulster Transport Authority also made an important contribution to the development of the DMU technology later applied by BR.

A cautionary word on the meanings of non-corridor, corridor and gangway is desirable, as usage in some highly respected books differs from the terms used by professional railwaymen. Three main types of vehicle emerged in steam days. The earliest was the compartment coach where the passenger was confined to the compartment he was sitting in until the vehicle reached a station. In some cases lavatories were added which could be reached from one compartment, or from several compartments by means of a side corridor. The next logical step was to add a flexible connection, which was called a gangway or corridor connection, from one coach to another. Possibly because the gangway between coaches was often called a corridor

connection, or maybe because most early gangwayed stock was built as compartment stock with a side corridor, the term corridor stock came to mean *any* vehicle with corridor connections. However open saloons had been built where there was no corridor as such, and from the 1900s, the side corridor compartment coach faced a challenge from the open layout with a centre aisle. To the casual observer a corridor coach with gangways could look just like an open coach with gangways, and both were often called corridor stock. If a vehicle did not have a corridor connection, railwaymen invariably called it non-corridor stock. This system was simple and easy to understand, provided you accepted its inherent faults.

Recent books on coaching stock have followed a different, but more consistent policy. The argument is that the term 'corridor coach' describes a vehicle with compartments, each of which opens on to a side passage or corridor. If there is a flexible connection at the end of the coach, permitting passengers to go through to the next vehicle, the coach is said to be gangwayed, as there is a gangway from coach to coach. The term open coach is not used in its original meaning of Second or Third class carriages that were open to the elements, but open internally, without partitions dividing the stock into compartments. Instead of compartments with a side corridor, there is a centre aisle with seats arranged each side of it. This difference is best grasped in the section on BR Standard Mk Is, where I have illustrated an FK, or gangwayed Corridor First, and an FO, a gangwayed open first. Both are gangwayed; one has a corridor, one has a central aisle and no corridor. Internally they are quite different, but from the outside, it would be easy to mistake an FK for an FO. In this system, a coach without a corridor connection is called non-gangwayed. This is a precise definition, but railwaymen call it non-corridor. In some ways this was unfortunate as some suburban stock was provided with a corridor to provide access to a lavatory, but without gangways to connect with adjacent coaches. These

By the dawn of the last century, rail travel for those fortunate enough to be able to afford to go First class had reached a degree of comfort scarcely surpassed even today. The London & North Western Railway 'American Special Stock' was exceptional even in that gilded age. The Atlantic liners to and from New York arrived and departed from Liverpool, and the LNWR carried American millionaires, actors and actresses, British nobility, foreign princes, businessmen and emigrants, between Euston and Liverpool (Riverside) station which adjoined the Landing Stage and the liners themselves. It was luxury and convenience far excelling anything that today's international air traveller might dream of. 65ft 6 in long 12-wheel carriages were introduced in 1908, staffed by immaculately turned out attendants. Intricately carved woodwork worthy of the most palatial mansion provided a degree of elegance that today's designers signally fail to achieve.

Above: Even before the 1955 Modernisation Plan had been printed, British Railways knew that the only way to contain costs on its vast network was to follow the lead of the Great Northern Railway of Ireland and the Ulster Transport Authority and introduce diesel multiple units. From 1954, a growing flood of DMUs swept steam away from much of the network. Enthusiasts of the day hated them, but in time the survivors were cherished as Heritage units, the last few surviving into the dawn of the new century. Alas, even with the economies of dieselisation, many lines were doomed by the more negative conclusions of the Beeching Report. One such route was the magnificent Great Central London Extension. M51677, 59661, 59762 and 51876 formed one of 41 four-car sets built for the Marylebone services in 1960. The set is on the 1.30pm Rugby to Marylebone on 3rd September 1966, the last day of operation of the London Extension as a through route. Later known as TOPS (Total Operations Processing System) class 115, they worked out of Liverpool, Tyseley and Marylebone until the 1990s. In their early days, they operated long distance services from Marylebone to Banbury and up the GC main line to Leicester, providing a high degree of comfort. They were amongst the best of the first generation DMUs.

vehicles were non-gangwayed corridor vehicles, but the term is so long that railwaymen called them lavatory stock. BR developed a telegraphic reporting code, in which First, Second and Third classes were F, S and T. Open stock had an O suffix, Corridor (that is, gangwayed) stock had a K suffix ('Korridor' 'perhaps!) and to use the term employed by BR itself, 'non corridor' stock had no suffix. The letters O, K or no suffix categorised the three types of vehicle. In deciding what system to follow, I have adopted a middle ground between the two, following enthusiast usage, yet respecting the terms used by professional railwaymen and adopted by BR itself. The rolling stock described in this volume was built in the days of the Imperial system of feet and inches. I have used the measurements that applied when the stock was built, as that is how it was known.

Once again, I would like to express my gratitude to my late father, Dr Robert Preston Hendry who encouraged my own interest in railways, and started the colour collection from which much that appears in these pages, is drawn. As with other volumes I have written, it is as much his book as mine. My sincere thanks go to Clive Partridge who first came to my father's model railway when we were at school together, joined BR and is now a senior Engineering Planning Manager on the railway. He provided a professional railway officer's perspective which has been most helpful. My wife Elena has got used to railway photographic trips, and is adept at spotting and filming the unusual. She has patiently accepted having the study piled knee-deep in drawings, photos and reference manuals for months on end.

In the Appendices, I have reproduced examples of the GWR, LMS and BR coach classification codes, including such rarities as a GWR FON! The way that trains are marshalled is important to the

modeller, so there is a selection of passenger train marshalling instructions. For the modeller of older stock, I have included a section on electric lighting in the early 1900s. In deciding what to include, I have used the same criteria that applied in the wagons or signalling volumes. As an active modeller, what information have I needed, but found difficult to locate? In our modelling work, I have been able to use the photo record my late father started, and I have pleasure in sharing it with you. I hope you find it as useful as I have.

Today we hear a lot about the alleged shortcomings of the rail network, but the reality is that thanks to generations of railway engineers, and the superb work of the Inspecting Officers of the old Board of Trade and later the Ministry of Transport, a British railway carriage is a very safe place indeed. The shortcomings are largely the result of political interference, which had begun in a modest way in the nineteenth century, and at that time had clear benefits. This degenerated into an inept politically inspired nationalisation in 1948 which converted the railways into a political football and an equally inept privatisation in the 1990s, which has created even more problems. The industry is now fragmented in a way that is demented, and is even more of a political football. The railway industry did a good job in taking the humble stagecoach and creating magnificent and safe passenger carriages. Given a level playing field, they could have done even better.

DESIGN, DETAILS AND BUILDERS

In this section, we will explore some of the design features and discuss some of the terminology that has been applied to coaching stock over the past century and a half.

Below: The earliest carriages were fitted with wooden bodies mounted on a separate wooden chassis. This consisted of longitudinal baulks of wood called solebars. These were secured by iron bolts and angle irons to transverse buffer beams or headstocks. The wheels were carried in axleboxes that were free to slide up and down vertical guides in the W-irons or axleguards. Springing was by rubber blocks and later by leaf springs, but they gave a harsh ride. Riding qualities were improved by connecting the springs to the chassis via shock absorbers. Nowadays hydraulic or air dampening is used, but in Victorian days, shock absorbers were often of rubber. A perimeter frame would have little resistance to deformation, so additional

transverse beams were fitted behind the headstocks and the midpoint, whilst diagonal timbers gave triangulation. Longitudinal and transverse metal tie rods, which were threaded at the ends to carry large nuts, tied the whole frame together. Composite Mansell wheels were common. In the Mansell wheel, the axle and tyre are of iron or steel, but are connected not by spokes or a steel disc, but by a wooden infill. This was thought to improve riding and reduce noise. As we can see, not all chassis were fitted with brakes. These two chassis, photographed at Douglas on 30th August 1966, were from a batch of over 50 4-wheelers built by the Metropolitan Railway Carriage & Wagon Co of Birmingham, for the opening of the Isle of Man Railway in 1873-74. Between 1909 and 1926 all were mounted in pairs on bogie chassis, releasing the 4-wheel chassis for use under freight stock. A few chassis were used as rail-carriers without any bodywork, giving a rare chance to study the construction of a mid-Victorian four wheel coach chassis. Although the centre chopper coupling is unique to the narrow gauge, the safety chains were a feature of Victorian coaching stock on standard gauge railways as well.

Bottom: The Metropolitan Railway Carriage & Wagon works was at Saltley in Birmingham, and until Wolverton works opened in 1865, had been the London & North Western Railway's carriage works. Few illustrations exist of pre-Wolverton LNWR coaching stock, but when I compared this photo of Isle of Man Railway passenger brake E5 of 1876 with contemporary engravings of early LNWR stock, the similarities were uncanny. The body panelling is unlike Wolverton designs, but is similar to pre 1865 LNWR stock built at Saltley, including the half round beading, square ended panels, and the deep waist panel. Long after the 'Saltley' body had vanished from the LNWR, its descendants survived in the Isle of Man. Equally remarkable is the livery. In the early 1900s, the IOMR enjoyed friendly relations with the Lancashire & Yorkshire Railway. LYR officers received free passes as a matter of course when holidaying on the island, and in return gave their expertise to their smaller neighbour across the water. Under Thomas Stowell, the IOMR manager from 1903 to 1927, the IOMR even adopted the two-tone brown livery of the LYR, though the scheme went out of fashion in the late 1920s. By that time E5 was out of regular use, and spent many years as a station store under the station canopy at Douglas. Protected from the elements it still carried 'LYR' colours when photographed in 1963. It survived until 1974.

Opposite page top: At first, 4-wheeled stock was universal, but as train speeds increased, its unsuitability for high speed running became clear. The solution was a longer 6-wheel chassis that would be steadier at higher speeds. The 6-wheeler became the dominant type from the 1860s until the dawn of the twentieth century. One of the few railways to remain faithful to the 6-wheeler after 1900 was the Belfast & County Down Railway, which turned out mid-Victorian 6-wheelers until the 1920s. The BCDR was absorbed into the Ulster Transport Authority in 1948, and route closures and dieselisation spelled the end for its archaic passenger carriages. However, the UTA required rail carriers, so stripped the bodies off several 6-wheelers. This chassis, although it bears no visible identity, is probably from BCDR First class saloon No 2 of 1916, which was converted to a rail carrier in 1954. It is of composite construction, a technique favoured by the BCDR, but uncommon elsewhere. It has steel solebars, but wooden headstocks and other frame members. The W irons are mounted outside the solebars, a design that was dropped in England by 1870, but which remained common in Ireland for another 50 years. Apart from permitting greater body length, another advantage of the 6-wheeler is apparent here. The solebar is supported at six points along its length. As the strength required in a beam varies with the unsupported distance, this permits a relatively light chassis. It has steel disc wheels. The wooden blocks and rails bolted above solebar height are a UTA addition to carry track panels. The chassis was photographed at Adelaide yard, Belfast on 21st August 1965.

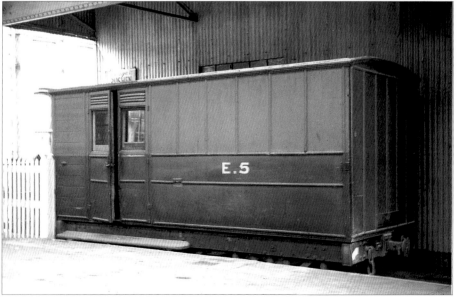

Right: Those of us who operate model railways will have seen this in model form, but perhaps never in real life, for this is the underside of a BR Mk I at Bury St Edmonds in May 1990. The coach had been tipped on its side for rescue service training, permitting some useful studies of the underside of a Mk I. Despite steel solebars, the chassis has substantial trussing due to the unsupported distance between bogie pivot points, 40ft on a 56ft 11in chassis, and 46ft 6in on a 63ft 5in chassis. In the foreground is one of the vacuum brake cylinders with its piston rod and transverse shaft. Nearby is the generator that charges the coach batteries, powered from the belt drive which is still in situ. Further along are the battery boxes and the vacuum brake cylinder for the far bogie.

Right: Most readers will have travelled on a Mk I in BR service or in preservation. Few will have seen the underside of a BR 'Commonwealth' bogie, let alone the discharge end of the roof drain or toilet discharge pipes! One problem with the Mk I bogie was that ride characteristics deteriorated after a relatively short spell in service, and after trials in 1955-58, a number of Mk Is were fitted with the heavy cast steel 'Commonwealth' bogies. These were costly to build and very heavy, but gave an excellent ride. Take a further look at the dynamo, the drive belt and the driving pulley on the inner axle of the bogie.

Below right: The names of the great company works such as Swindon, Derby or Doncaster are well known, as are private locomotive builders such as Beyer Peacock, Kitson or Hunslet. Some cities are renowned for their locomotives, but few enthusiasts would put Birmingham high on the list of railway suppliers. In fact, the West Midlands became a major producer of passenger and freight stock at the dawn of the railway age. Located close together between Birmingham and the outskirts of Wolverhampton, the builders developed a wealth of expertise that fuelled the growth of the trade. They included the Birmingham Railway Carriage & Wagon Co, Brown Marshalls & Co Ltd, Joseph Wright & Sons, later to become Metropolitan Railway Carriage & Wagon Ltd, Midland Railway Carriage & Wagon Ltd, The Oldbury Railway Carriage & Wagon Co, Patent Shaft & Axletree and the Staffordshire Wheel & Axle Co. Eventually many of these companies were merged into Metropolitan, which became associated with the engineering giants Vickers and Cammell Laird to form Metropolitan Cammell Carriage & Wagon Co Ltd. All were proud to put their makers plates on their products, but none eclipsed Metropolitan in style. This example from 1923 gives the then title of the company, The Metropolitan Carriage, Wagon & Finance Co Ltd. Today we are used to finance companies in the motor or domestic appliance trades, enabling us to buy goods on hire purchase. Many of the carriage and wagon builders of the past offered a similar service to their customers.

Left: W890W was a corridor Third built to GWR diagram C82 under Lot 1714 at Swindon in 1948, and is depicted at Dringhouses in February 1967. In this view we can see the gangway (or corridor connection) and electrical and vacuum connections, axleboxes, door fittings and other details of GWR Hawksworth period stock. Modellers should note the gap between the W and the numerals.

Above: Continuing with the Great Western, we will look at the centre door on this late period auto coach. Stock from Diagrams A38 and A43 was built in BR days between 1951 and 1954, but was essentially GW. Although taken in evening sunlight, which adds warmth to the exposure, the way in which the solebars, bogie frames and truss rods have picked up dust and rust is apparent. Except when a vehicle was 'ex works', the one colour you did not see below the bodywork was the glossy black beloved of modellers. Note the oil blackening around the springs, axleboxes, vacuum cylinder and brake shaft bearings. Attention to weathering details can transform a model from a technically excellent but unconvincing miniature, into a plausible replica of the real thing.

Right: Doyen of the coachbuilders was Joseph Wright, a leading stage carriage proprietor in pre-railways days, owning and building many vehicles for the London to Birmingham run. Seeing the writing on the wall for his old business, Wright set up a railway coach building works in London in 1840, but moved to Birmingham in 1845. Within a few years, he could claim to be, 'carriage builder to the world'. One of the most fantastic emanations from the works was a state carriage built for Abbas Pasha, Khedive of Egypt in 1858. With an 11ft wheelbase, it was 24ft 10in over buffers, and the overall height to the top of the central crown was 15ft 5in. It may have been shipped out as a set of parts and assembled locally by Wright's staff, or it could have been dispatched by rail, minus the crowns no doubt, as practice varied. I have included it here as it is the earliest known example of a Wright coach in colour.It reminds us of the major contribution of British companies to the development of the railways of the world. Of practical importance to British modellers, the underframe, despite its decorative overlay, is standard Wright/Saltley practice, with the rudimentary horn guides bolted to the outside face of the solebars, tie rods connecting the axle guards and diagonal tie rods giving additional bracing at the ends. The flat springs with very few leaves are typical of this period, as are the thin buffer spindles and safety chains. In 1862, the company became the Metropolitan Railway Carriage & Wagon Co. It was still sufficiently proud of this vehicle to include it in their brochures over 50 years later.

Below: Oldbury lies midway between Birmingham and Wolverhampton, and was home to the Oldbury Railway Carriage & Wagon Co. Taken into the Metropolitan fold before the First World War, Oldbury had been previously known as the Railway Carriage Company, and had a chequered history with at least two financial reconstructions. Donegal Railway No 30, seen in Strabane station yard, was built by Oldbury in 1901 as a twin saloon Third with open verandas. These were later boarded in and the coach was converted to run as a trailer with the pioneering County Donegal Railways Joint Committee diesel railcars. It survived up to the closure of the CDRJC at the end of 1959, and was bought by an American, Dr Ralph Cox, but was never shipped to the States. Instead it fell prey to vandals and was later scrapped.

COACHING STOCK IN SERVICE

Coaching Stock was built to carry passengers or high value commodities, such as fish, milk or mails, reasonably quickly. Unlike freight trains where there were seven basic types of service ranging from the fully fitted express goods to the humble 'pick up', stopping at all stations, there were just four basic types of passenger train. The first of these was the express which travelled long distances with few intermediate stops, and was expected to average not less than 40mph. Next was the ordinary stopping passenger train, which might call at selected stations or all stations, and usually ran from one large town or junction to the next. The push-pull, auto train or motor, was a variety of ordinary passenger train in which the locomotive and stock were equipped so that the driver could control the regulator and vacuum brakes from the leading coach when the engine was propelling the train. Empty coaching stock, could comprise any type of passenger stock including an empty steam rail motor or an electrical multiple unit. The final type of train complying with coaching stock requirements was the fish, fruit, newspaper, parcels or mail train, which ran at passenger train speeds, but did not carry passengers.

Below: Some modellers seem to think that the railways marshalled stock almost at random. In fact, carriages normally worked in fixed rakes, and selecting the right stock for each rake was a complex business requiring knowledge of the passenger mix, line restrictions and the pluses and minuses of individual types of stock. The flood of Mk Is from 1951 and of DMUs from the mid-fifties permitted BR to withdraw many of the elderly pre-group coaches that had come from the Big Four in 1948. By the early sixties, the only place on BR where complete rakes of pre-grouping passenger stock hauled by matching engines could be seen, was in the Isle of Wight. A former London & South Western Railway Adams O2 class 0-4-4T, No w24 *Calbourne*, enters Ryde St John's Road station with an up train from Ventnor on 21st May 1964. The six coach train is a mixture of ex South Eastern & Chatham Railway and London, Brighton & South Coast Railway non-corridor stock, which had survived on the island because the newer Mk I stock was too large for the clearances in Ryde tunnel. At this time, there were eleven passenger sets on the island. In winter, they were made up into 3-car sets with a brake 2nd at each end and a composite in the middle. The brake at the Ryde end was ordinarily a four compartment ex-SECR vehicle, as here. This was due to its greater luggage capacity compared to the six or seven compartment ex-Brighton brakes. On a holiday line with ship to train transfers at Ryde Pier Head, the proximity of the bigger luggage compartment to the boat was important. In summer, the Ryde-Ventnor sets were strengthened to six vehicles with additional 2nds or sometimes two 2nds and one

composite. With ex-Chatham and ex-Brighton stock to add to the sets, marshalling considerations again prevailed. The Ventnor trains were more heavily patronised than the Cowes services, and as Brighton stock was lighter than SECR stock, but carried more passengers, it was preferred on the Ventnor trains. With the exception of the third vehicle, the rest of the stock on this train is ex-LBSCR, as one would expect. This is a classic case of practical railwaymen using their knowledge of their stock and of their traffic.

Opposite page top: GWR 61xx, 'large prairie', No 6143 heads a three coach rake along the GW & GC Joint Line near Saunderton in 1962. This shows a different way of marshalling a three coach non-corridor local set, for unlike the basic IoW set with a brake at each end and a composite in the centre, there is a single brake with the guard's compartment at the inward end of the set. On a suburban service like this, few passengers would take luggage, so seating capacity is more important than luggage space. One way to achieve this is to use a single brake. Sometimes this would be the end coach, but it could also be the centre coach, which provides a more symmetrical set. The leading coach is an LMS Diagram D1964 non-corridor Brake Second with two pairs of double doors on the van section. The second vehicle is a BR Mk I nine compartment Second built to Diagram 326. Differences in the heights of the livery bands are apparent, whilst the third vehicle, a nine compartment First/Second composite is devoid of lining. This set would have been useless for the IoW but is ideal here.

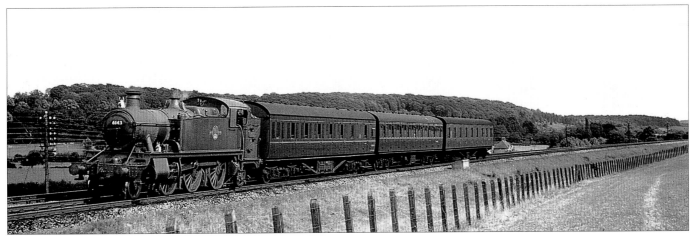

Right: If we are to model passenger services convincingly, we should pay attention to the ancillary activities. Enthusiasts seldom record such scenes, and when it is too late, and we want to recreate the scene, we wonder what it was like. This study of Gloucester in July 1976 shows stock in Rail blue and grey, with a Mk I BG in the background. A passenger's luggage has been unloaded from the BG, and the guard, who already has his green flag in his hand, is about to close the doors. In the foreground is a yellow liveried Post Office tractor unit, XFH784H with ER lettering and royal crown, a post office mail trolley, and a blue liveried BR 'brute', parcels cage. With the change to new uniforms since privatisation, even the dress of the guard is now of historic interest, whilst the livery of the post office driver could be described as suntanned, for this was the long hot summer of 1976 when the government eventually found it necessary to appoint a minister for drought. Within a few days, the skies opened, and the drought was over. It was one of the most successful ministerial appointments in history!

Below: Many modellers feel that an express train in the steam age had to be ten or more coaches in length, but this delightful early evening portrait shows a train more suited to the average layout. A Banbury based Stanier Black Five, No 44860, arrives at Rugby Central at 6.39pm, with the 4.38pm from Marylebone to Nottingham Victoria on 15th October 1965. With the run-down of the GC, the passenger service was being cut to the bone, and the train is scheduled to make six stops in the 57 miles between Woodford Halse and Nottingham. By this time, LNER stock had vanished from the GC section and passenger sets were made up of Mk Is, as in this case, or some of the last surviving LMS gangwayed stock. The set consists of the classic BSK, CK, SK, BSK formation.

Top: A rebuilt Bulleid 'Merchant Navy' pacific, No 35028 *Clan Line*, enters Salisbury with the down Atlantic Coast Express on 13th April 1961. Leaving Waterloo with a full-length formation, the ACE was renowned for the manner in which it shed portions at regular intervals on its journey along the Southern main line across Devon and Cornwall. At the time of this photo, the train left Waterloo at 11.00am and conveyed through carriages to Padstow, Bude, Plymouth, Ilfracombe, Torrington, Exmouth and Sidmouth. It was a monument to the British *through coach* that was a godsend to travellers with heavy holiday luggage or children, but fell victim to the Beeching era retreat from summer Saturday holiday traffic. The normal express train at this period would consist of Full Brakes or Brake Seconds at the ends, Seconds and Composites and perhaps a First or a Restaurant car. Because of its fragmentation into seven separate portions, each of which required brake accommodation for the guard and for passengers' luggage, plus First and Second class accommodation, the ACE contained an exceptionally high proportion of composites and brakes.

Above: A Saltley based Stanier Black Five No 44777 starts out after a signal check at Banbury in 1965 at the head of a parcels train. The leading vehicle is a BR Mk I GUV bogie van built to Diagram 811. Further down the train is the usual mix of stock, including a CCT, an LMS BG, and many other varieties of equipment. Virtually any combination of stock could be seen from the 1950s to the 1970s, with differing body styles, heights, roof profiles and liveries. As a result, parcels trains were some of the most interesting services to model, especially as parcels stock tended to outlast contemporary passenger carriages.

Below: This evocative study of Kyle of Lochalsh dates from June 1972, and reveals that other than for the change of motive power and of livery, train operations in the early years of the post-steam British Rail were little affected. Apart from a Scottish Region Type 2 with a tablet catcher recess (needed in the days before radio electronic token block), the train consists of a BR 4-wheel CCT to Diagram 816, a Southern passenger luggage van, which could hardly get much further from home and five gangwayed BR Mk Is. On the left beyond the platform are two BGs, one of LMS ancestry, one of BR origin, and to the right is a Shocvan, recognisable by its three vertical white stripes. The ferry in the background was David MacBrayne's newest acquisition at the time, the 1970 built MV *Iona* of 1192 grt (gross register tons). Transferred to the MacBrayne fleet in 1972, it came up from the Clyde to Mallaig and Kyle for the Stornoway service. An idea of the integrated nature of transport in the Western Highlands at that time is given by the MacBrayne trailer visible to the right of the passenger stock.

Bottom: Railway preservation in Britain began with the narrow gauge Talyllyn Railway in 1951. Standard gauge preservation got off the ground about ten years later with the Middleton Railway in Leeds and the Bluebell Railway in Sussex. It was a race against time to raise finance to buy the lines, and to buy and restore suitable stock. Many classes of locomotive did not make it into preservation. Two obvious omissions are the GWR 10xx 'County' class and the magnificent 68xx 'Grange'. Where engines and stock were preserved, it was often a chance affair, and there was seldom money to buy sets of matching carriages. Many pioneer preservationists also felt it was necessary to create a preservation image, for who would come to look at engines in BR colours. As a result, preserved trains were some of the most colourful and variegated in railway history. For the modeller, it gives amazing opportunities, yet is seldom tackled, which is a pity. Many of us have a favourite period or company, but we like engines from outside our period or area. We run them and feel guilty, or do not run them

and feel sad. With a preservation layout, almost anything is possible. You could double head a BR 9F with an LNWR 2-4-0, and if there is a connection with BR, a blue-liveried Class 86 could pass by on an adjacent track. I have seen just such a combination. Viewers of that wonderful film, *The Railway Children,* will recognise this next location, it is the Keighley & Worth Valley Railway and this view dates from 15th April 1973. The locomotive is the KWVR's J94 0-6-0ST *Fred*. The leading coach is an ex Metropolitan Railway vehicle, with Southern, BR and LMS stock further down the train. No two vehicles are the same, nor do any two carry the same livery. On any normal layout, it would look unconvincing, but this is how it was. Services on preserved lines are often intensive, with lots of shunting as well, so there is plenty of operational potential, especially if you model a steam gala weekend!

Top: In the days when most consignments moved by rail, a fleet of parcels vehicles built to coaching stock requirements, was created. Often enjoying far longer lives than their passenger counterparts, the variety of stock at a parcels depot was amazing. This view of the former GWR Wolverhampton (Low Level) station dates from 2nd July 1976, and shows the station after the demise of the old GWR Paddington to Birkenhead line as a through route. The section from Birmingham to Wolverhampton was closed, and passenger services transferred to the nearby ex-LNWR Wolverhampton (High Level) station. The lines north of Low Level were lifted, and the former station, now in use as a parcels depot, could only be reached from the south end. The stock includes BR Mk I BGs, Southern passenger luggage vans, Diagram 811 GUVs, and M94257, a Diagram 816 CCT. This was a typical mix of stock at the time. With the retreat from rail parcels distribution, the tracks have been lifted, but these fine old station buildings have been preserved.

Above: In pre-grouping days, coaching stock was worked out from the big city stations to carriage depots, some distance away, for servicing. This included internal and external cleaning and the refilling water tanks. Many carriage sheds survived at the end of the steam era, but were a dying breed by then. At Vauxhall station, the LNWR carriage depot for the Birmingham area adjoined the platforms. It has been re-roofed with a modern lightweight roof, but the walls are original, as are the raised walkways between each track. They were used by cleaners, as passenger stock was hand cleaned before spray washer plants came into use. Inside the shed, the roads were provided with pits, and a carriage examiner can be seen in a high visibility track jacket, near the left hand edge of the shed. Water hoses, for cleaning purposes and topping up toilet tanks were provided, and some hoses are visible near the supports for the cleaning platforms. Before electric lighting became the norm, oil lamps might require changing or gas reservoirs refilling, before the next journey.

1830-1900
THE FORMATIVE YEARS

The period from 1830 to 1900 saw the railway carriage develop from diminutive four-wheelers that showed their road stagecoach origins to well-designed, robust and elegant stock. It was a period of astonishing technical innovation. Four wheelers were universal at the beginning, but by 1900, 6-wheel or bogie stock predominated. In 1830, timber was used for bodies and frames. By 1900 steel chassis were normal, although timber remained customary for bodywork. The earliest stock was often unbraked, or provided with a crude hand brake. By 1900, the continuous automatic brake was compulsory and gas or electric lighting had replaced candles or oil lamps.

Right: Today we take personal mobility for granted. A train takes us hundreds of miles in a few hours. By car we go where we want at will, but for thousands of years, if mankind wanted to go to the next village or town, he walked, or if he was wealthy, he went on horseback. In living memory, there were people who had never left the parish they had been born in. The first step in this transformation was confined to royalty and the nobility. Queen Elizabeth 1 had one of the first carriages in the British Isles. By the 1650s, there were a few slow and primitive stage carriages providing an infrequent service for the traveller to use if he could afford the fare. Journeys were measured in days, and with increasing traffic, the roads of the day, which had never been good, deteriorated. Turnpike trusts were set up from 1663, but it was not until 1700 that turnpikes started to multiply. In return for making up the road, the turnpike trust levied tolls on road users. By 1776, the coach journey from London to Edinburgh took just four days. The first Royal Mail stagecoach ran in 1784, setting new standards of speed and efficiency. It was this network of stagecoaches, some run for the General Post Office, others by private contractors, that existed at the dawn of the railway age. By trial and error, the coachbuilders had discovered what worked, and what failed, for the roads were rough, potholed and a formidable challenge for any vehicle. This early nineteenth century print, from a painting by James Pollard, recalls the stagecoach with its covered body with a rounded base, side doors and a single droplight in the door. The driver was mounted up front, and poorer passengers travelled outside, along with a guard, whose duties included fighting off highwaymen, for Dick Turpin and his confreres were real enough. When the first railways came to be built, it was to the road coachbuilders that they looked for expertise in designing carriages to run on the iron road.

Bottom: When the Liverpool & Manchester Railway opened in 1830, the railway carriage was still a novelty, and the L&M had to blaze the trail. The coachbuilders had learned to build reliable and long lasting road coaches, and it was to one of the foremost builders that George Stephenson went. Thomas Clarke Worsdell had been apprenticed to Howe & Shanks of London, and in 1813 set up his own business as a coachbuilder, moving to Liverpool in 1827. The following year he was asked to build the tender for the *Rocket*, and carriages for the as yet unfinished L&M. Worsdell used his road coaching background to produce a stagecoach on flanged wheels. With a seven foot wheelbase, such vehicles were very unsteady. In 1836, T C Worsdell was succeeded by his son Nathaniel, who, in 1837, invented the first Travelling Post Office apparatus for picking up and dropping mailbags at speed. In 1838, Nathaniel built the *Enterprise* coach for the L&M, in which he united three stagecoach bodies on a single underframe, creating a compartment coach. Despite this revolutionary step, the old established decorative ideas were so ingrained, that Worsdell retained the moulding lines of the stagecoach. *Experience* also dated from this period on the Liverpool & Manchester Railway. Early coaches had either no buffers or horsehair buffers, but crude spring buffers soon appeared. As coaches were loose coupled by chains, it must have been a bumpy ride. This early coach has no brakes. If required, a chock or sprag was put against one of the wheels. In the days of the stagecoach, the guard travelled outside, and wooden seats and foot rests were provided at the ends of these newfangled railway carriages so that the guard could occupy his traditional post. Buffeted by the winds, drenched by rain and seared by cinders, it must have been a revolting job. No surprisingly, the idea of a separate guards van soon evolved. Apart from offering better conditions, it allowed the guard to do his paperwork on the move, saving time at stations. It permitted him to keep an eye on luggage and parcels, and provided with a brake wheel, he could make some contribution towards stopping the train.

A CARRIAGE OF THE FIRST CLASS
L & M RY. 1838.

Left: The Festiniog Railway was built in the 1830s to convey slate, and its first passenger carriages did not come from Brown Marshalls until 1864-67. Rescued for preservation in the 1950s, four of these venerable boxes were restored to running order. Carriages 3,4,5 and 6 were photographed at Portmadoc Harbour station on 9th August 1960, along with brake van No 2. Built with longitudinal seats on the centreline of the coach, often called knifeboard seats, they were very crude. They included panelled and matchboarded enclosed carriages, and a half-open Observation car. The low-slung design, with the wheels obscured by the body, was due to the restricted FR loading gauge. Other than for popularising the narrow gauge, these archaic vehicles had no impact on coaching stock design, as the main line companies were already far in advance of such equipment.

Centre left: The preserved railways have now been around longer than the 'Big Four' of the grouping era. They also offer wonderful opportunities to the modeller, as is evidenced by this venerable four-wheeler on the IoW Steam Railway seen in 1995. It was built c1864 at the Bow works of the North London Railway as a four compartment First. In December 1897 it came to the Isle of Wight Railway via a second hand rolling stock dealer N Jones. It became IWR No 46, and one compartment was downgraded to Second class. It would have become SR 6336, but was withdrawn in 1926. It became a bungalow on Hayling Island for the next half century, returning to the Isle of Wight in 1975. Using a shortened underframe from a Southern CCT, it re-entered service in 1986. Initially it ran in IWR varnished livery, but was repainted in SR green to match other vintage stock. Although this vehicle was withdrawn prior to being renumbered, so never carried this livery in service, this superb rendering of the Maunsell era SR livery should be useful to modellers. Unlike the panelled Festiniog coach we have seen in the previous view, there is no waist panel, the beading running from the window level to the bottom of the cladding. The NLR was one of the few companies to favour this style. Rakes of more modern four-wheelers survived until electrification by the LNWR shortly before the grouping. The doors are hung to the left. The frames of the 'droplights', or windows, in the doors that could be lowered, were often varnished rather than painted the body colour.

Bottom left: Two different ways exist to build wooden bodied carriages or wagons. The planking or sheeting can be fitted to the outside of the wooden frames, creating an inside framed vehicle, or the planking can be on the inside of the framework, which is then exposed to view. Stagecoach builders adopted the neater finish of an internally framed vehicles, but farm carts were often externally framed. This division lasted into railway days, with many early wagons being outside framed. Stockton & Darlington Railway No 179, a four-wheeled

Continued on next page

Third Open built at Darlington in 1867 displays the constructional features of an externally framed passenger carriage. The THIRD CLASS inscription is not carried on the doors, but on the panelling between doors. The doors are right hinged, as with the early FR vehicles, whilst the coach is fitted with oil lamp pots, split spoke wheels and wooden brake blocks worked from a wheel in the right hand compartment. Today we are used to self-locking droplights in doors, but in Victorian times, a leather strap was provided with a series of holes. The droplight frame rested on a raised ledge, and to open the window, it was lifted clear of this by means of the strap and then lowered as far as desired and the strap secured through one of the small holes on to a knob on the door frame. As the right hand door is open, the strap and the mode of operation is clearly visible. No 179 was sold to the Forncett Railway but eventually preserved at York. It was rebuilt at Shildon, where it is on display in 1975.

Top: E900270E, seen at York in April 1967, began life as NER No 1173. It was built as a First class family saloon by the NER at York in 1870, but was re-designated an officers inspection saloon in 1892, and used by Phillip Burt, Superintendent of the Line. In 1911 it was transferred to the District Engineer, Hull, and became LNER No 21173 in 1925. In 1963 it was transferred to the Civil Engineer York, and is seen in service in April 1967 shortly before withdrawal. The vehicle beyond E900270E is a BR Mk I horsebox, E96305, converted for CCE use as staff coach DE321107 in 1966. It is still in its all over Engineering green livery. Later it would sport a two-tone yellow and green scheme. It may be that this was a trial run with the new staff coach, with the venerable NER saloon going out on its final trip. Beyond the

Mk I horsebox is a tunnel gauge wagon, and a Type 2 diesel. This is a wonderful time warp with an 1870s coach and a 1960s locomotive in service together. After withdrawal, E900270E went to the Keighley & Worth Valley Railway.

Above: Four wheel carriages varied from 20 to 30 feet over the body, and on the generous curves on the standard gauge lines, this provided reasonable riding qualities. On the narrow gauge lines, where sharper curves prevailed, long vehicles might suffer from clearance problems, and the long rigid wheelbase could bind on curves. As a result, 4 wheelers were shorter, with adverse effects on their riding. The greater width of narrow gauge stock compared to the track gauge exacerbated this problem. The far-sighted Festiniog manager

and engineer, C E Spooner, began sketching out longer bogie vehicles in 1870, and Brown Marshalls built the first pair of FR bogie coaches, Nos 15 and 16 in 1871. Remarkably they were carried on channel section wrought iron underframes. This combination of bogie stock and iron underframes placed the FR at the forefront of British coaching stock design. Two more coaches, Nos 17 and 18, appeared in 1876. Because of the restricted loading gauge, the body was low mounted, with the bogies largely hidden behind the solebars. End platforms with railings were provided to enable passengers to cross from one side of the train to the other. No 17 is seen at Portmadoc Harbour station in 2001. The body style with its rounded panels is typical of mid-Victorian design.

Left: When the Peel and Port Erin lines of the Isle of Man Railway opened in 1873 and 1874, the railway was equipped with over fifty four-wheel carriages. Partly this was because funds had been tight and four-wheelers were simple and cheap to build, and did not push technology to the limits. Even so, it was a mistake, for the IMR was unlike the Welsh slate lines, where slow train speeds prevailed. IMR passenger trains ran at similar speeds to the mainland, and the 16ft 6 in and 17ft 6in four wheelers ran appallingly. By January 1875, the IMR manager and engineer F H Trevithick, had obtained quotes from Brown Marshalls, Ashbury and Metropolitan for 35 foot long bogie stock. Brown Marshalls received the contract and F1-F6 entered service prior to the 1876 season. They were six compartment vehicles, one end compartment having a brake wheel for the guard. The brake shaft ran outside the end of the coach, and the wheel was mostly housed in a sheet iron casing bolted to the end of the bodywork. A wooden door permitted the wheel to be closed off, so passengers could use the compartment when not required by the guard. The early IMR bogie stock was straight sided, and the cladding was carried down to mask the solebars. In common with the NLR coach, the lower beading runs from window level to the bottom of the cladding, but there was no bottom horizontal bead, and just one intermediate bead between each pair of compartments. An ornate cast iron Brown Marshalls makers' plate, featuring the municipal arms of Birmingham, was fitted to the solebar. F4 is depicted at Douglas in May 1967.

Centre left: Many writers have castigated unimaginative Victorian engineers for adopting 6-wheel rather than bogie designs. In fact the Victorian engineers were highly practical men. The load a beam can bear varies as to the length of the unsupported span. A 30ft long 6-wheel chassis is supported by three wheel sets equally spaced out, instead of a pair of bogies near the ends of the carriage. A bogie coach had a heavier underframe and heavy bogies. It cost more to build, haul and repair. That is why the 6-wheeler was so popular, but its long rigid wheelbase was unsuited to lines with sharp curves. James Cleminson had the answer. He patented a flexible 6-wheel chassis in 1876. The centre axle was carried in a truck that was free to move sideways on sliding bearings. The outer axles were also carried in trucks, which were secured to the chassis by a bogie pivot, permitting them to rotate. Longitudinal beams projected from the trucks, and were connected at the extremities by a double-hinged joint that was the key to the whole system working. As the leading axle entered a curve, it pivoted, causing the leading truck beam to move radially. This caused the centre truck to slide sideways, which imparted a turning movement to the rear truck. Transition from straight to curve and back, was dealt with through the double hinges. In this rare study of the Cleminson trucks from IMR coach No N41, taken at Douglas on 1st June 1967, we see the trucks themselves, the longitudinal frame and the hinged joints.

Previous page bottom: Prior to opening in 1879, the Manx Northern Railway ordered 14 Cleminson six-wheelers from the Swansea Wagon Co Ltd. They were 30 feet over the body, and because the support points for the trucks meant an unsupported span of less than 7 feet, compared to the 25ft 8 in of an IOMR bogie coach, they could be lightly built, saving capital costs, and reducing train tare weights. Ninety years later, the Cleminsons showed no signs of frame sag unlike the IMR timber framed bogie stock which had a pronounced sag! How did they ride? Some authors have castigated the Cleminson system as unsteady. In 1975, I was involved in preserving MNR No 3, later IMR N42. Cleminson stock had last run in passenger service in the 1940s, but I was invited to travel in the coach when it was moved by rail from Castletown to Port Erin. The other passengers included my mother and the family dog. The ride was far superior to IOMR bogie stock. Archer's faith was not misplaced. No 3 is seen in undercoat prior to entering the Port Erin Railway Museum in 1976.

Top right: The first section of what became the County Donegal Railways Joint Committee's lines, from Strabane to Stranorlar, was opened in 1863 using the Irish broad gauge of 5ft 3in. It was re-built in the 1890s to the 3ft gauge as extensions to the system were being built to that gauge. For the reopening of the line and its extension to Killybegs, 17 bogie carriages were delivered from Oldbury in 1893. Five, Nos 12 and 14-17 were tri-composites, with a 2/2/1/1/3 arrangement. They were built with matchboarded straight sides, an unusual form of construction for this period. Many railways progressed from oil lighting to gas and then electric lighting for its coaching stock, but the CDRJC opted for acetylene lighting. This archaic system survived into the 1950s, and the red box on the end of CDJC No 14 is the acetylene generator. Acetylene gas is produced when a small amount of water is added to Calcium Carbide in a mixing vessel. The gas is not stored, as with ordinary coal gas, but burnt immediately in suitable burners to produce an intense light. Many early motorcars used Acetylene headlamps. Its main drawback is that the smell can be pungent. No 14 was auctioned in 1961 after the closure of the CDRJC in 1959.

Bottom: From the 1860s, when it became clear that the Great Western Railway's broad gauge was doomed, the GWR entered into a quarter-century slumber, which ended only when the inevitable but sad abolition of the broad gauge took effect in 1892. In the years to come, the GWR changed from being relatively backward to adopting the cutting edge reforms of George Jackson Churchward. On 24th August 1894, Swindon works received orders to build a 56ft bogie directors' saloon with large compartments at each end and a central kitchen compartment. No 249, a Brake First Open to Diagram G3 (Lot 745), made a trial trip on 22nd October 1894, less than two months after the order for its construction had been given. It was used in the GWR royal train when required, but could also be used for track inspections, with an external seat fitted to either end. In 1907 it became No 8249, and then No 9045 in the Special Saloons series. In 1940, it was sent to Plymouth as the District Inspection Saloon, and numbered 80978. Little used, it was still in chocolate and cream livery when withdrawn in 1963 as W80978W. Two years of storage followed, until it was preserved on the Dart Valley Railway. It is seen at Buckfastleigh in July 1966. The unusual roof profile, with the clerestory swept down to meet the overhung roof, had appeared on a Brake Composite in 1892, and No 249 was only the second vehicle to receive it.

1900-1922
THE AGE OF ELEGANCE

As the Victorian era drew to a close, the railways of Britain entered a golden age. The graceful late nineteenth century engines were soon to be supplanted by newer and more powerful machines from designers such as George Jackson Churchward, George Whale and J G Robinson. Coaching stock was set to make a similar leap forward from traditional Victorian four and six wheelers or short bogie stock, to high roofed carriages that could be 65 or even 70 foot long. Ornate panelling and liveries characterised the magnificent stock of this period.

Right: Though progress was in the air, this vehicle could have been built at any time in the previous 30 years. Even by Irish standards, the Dundalk, Newry & Greenore Railway was unusual. Owned by the mighty LNWR, the DNGR was an Irish broad gauge version of the 'Premier Line', equipped with a batch of Ramsbottom 'Special' tanks built for the 5ft 3in Irish gauge, and rakes of LNWR style six-wheelers. DNGR coach No 1 was a replacement for an earlier carriage, and was built at Wolverton in 1901. It was a First/Second composite with a steel underframe, and was pure LNWR, except that the Hibernia transfer of the DNGR replaced the Britannia transfer of the LNWR. When the DNGR closed, No 1 was preserved in 1952, and is seen in the Belfast Transport Museum on 1st September 1964.

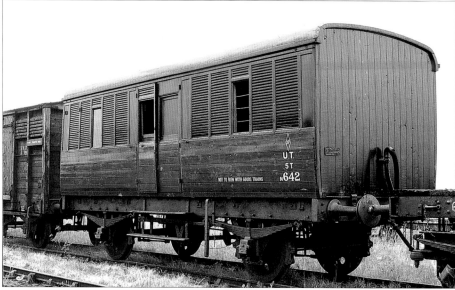

Centre: Victorian and Edwardian railway enthusiasts travelling to the Emerald Isle were often surprised by the marked similarities between the Great Northern Railway (Ireland) and its English counterpart. This was largely due to James Crawford Park, the GNR(I) locomotive superintendent. Park had trained at Crewe, and had moved to Doncaster in 1866, where he became head of the drawing office under Archibald Sturrock and then Patrick Stirling. To what extent Park may have helped shape the Stirling look is unclear, but when he moved to the Ireland in 1881, he took the Doncaster locomotive and carriage look with him, and gracefully proportioned apple green locomotives and elegant coaching stock became the hallmark of the Irish company. GNR(I) No 759 was a Y4 ventilated van with louvered sides built at Dundalk works in 1901. At the break up of the GNR in 1958, when the assets of the railway were split between the CIE in Eire and the Ulster Transport Authority in Northern Ireland, No 759 acquired the dark green livery of the UTA, becoming N642 in the unified stock list developed by the UTA Chief Mechanical Engineer, J H Houston. GN stock carried a small cast iron plate on the ends giving the vehicle type and overall dimensions. In this case, 24ft 0ins x 8ft 9in, with a tare weight of 9 tons. N642 is seen at Adelaide yard Belfast on 21st August 1965.

Above: The combination of LNWR livery and an LMS carriage transfer seems incongruous, but is historically correct. This Corridor Brake First was built in 1905-06 to Diagram 127 with a 'cove' roof. In 1913, it was renumbered 5624. In 1924, it was transferred to royal train duties, and received a clerestory roof to match other royal stock when it was renumbered 10070 in 1925. When the newly formed LMS management informed His Majesty King George V that they planned to repaint the former LNWR royal train into standard LMS crimson lake, the King objected strongly, and the royal train

continued to carry LNWR colours, but with LMS lettering, hence the curious combination on this vehicle. In 1925 the brake compartment was rebuilt to receive two diesel generators to provide electric lighting for the royal train when it was stabled overnight. The carriage became No 5154 under the 1933 LMS scheme, and in 1937 received a replacement LMS steel chassis. It continued in royal train use until 1977, and was handed over to the NRM in 1978, becoming a part of the reserve collection.

Right: Two attendants compartments were provided with buttoned leather door cladding.

Below: The combination of the LMS crest on LNWR colours merits a closer look.

Opposite page bottom: By the 1960s, non-passenger carrying stock of comparable age was rare on BR, so I was delighted to discover this grounded GWR body at Hartlebury on 2nd July 1976. It is a Diagram N9 horsebox , or 'Paco' in the GWR telegraph reporting code. This diagram originated around 1901, but was a development of the 1880s N5 design. It was 17 feet over the body overhang, and would have been mounted on an 11-foot wheelbase chassis. The end window is a later addition, but the nearside is little altered from service days. Grounded vehicles such as this survived into the modern traction era, and can add a welcome touch of diversity to a 1970s layout. In its working life, it would have been a regular sight on the back of passenger trains ranging from branch and local workings, to main line expresses. As a child in the 1950s, I can recall horseboxes in use, and it was only in the 1960s that this source of traffic finally collapsed. The short sidings with side and end loading docks often found at one end of a station were intended for horse boxes and carriage trucks, and this kind of traffic adds much to the operating interest on any layout.

Left: M36757M is an LNWR Diagram D445A CCT, or four-wheel covered combination truck with end and side doors and ventilation louvres. It could be used for motor vehicles loaded via the end doors or for milk, fish, perishables or parcels traffic loaded via the side doors. With a 12-foot wheelbase, it could run in passenger trains and was a versatile and useful design. Wolverton turned out many CCTs in 1907-1909, and they were placed in the 36xxx series by the LMS under its 1933 re-numbering scheme. Many were withdrawn in the 1930s, but a number survived to carry BR lettering. The last example was withdrawn from revenue service in December 1956, but a few survived in departmental service. Mostly these were repainted, but M36757M was still in faded BR coaching stock livery when spotted at Wolverton works in 1969.

Centre left: Another vehicle that retained obsolete colours was W80977W, seen in BR carmine and cream a decade after the livery was discontinued. Built at the Ashbury railway carriage works in Manchester in 1895 for the Manchester & Milford Haven Railway. At first sight, it is logical that a local manufacturer should build a coach for a Manchester line. However the M&MH served neither Manchester nor Milford Haven, but struck south from Aberystwyth into the wilderness of rural Wales. The company limped along, its dreams of trunk line status shattered, until it was taken into the Great Western fold. This coach became GWR 7900 in 1906, was withdrawn two years later and fitted with a new body at Swindon in 1910 to Diagram Q1, becoming. No 6479. Initially at Taunton, it became the Gloucester Division Inspection Saloon. It received carmine and cream livery in BR days, and was in service until the early sixties. Its limited use meant that it never went into any later BR livery. W80977W is seen in June 1966 at Buckfastleigh, soon after its arrival for preservation on the Dart Valley Railway.

Previous page bottom: DE320709 shows a very different style of coach building. It is one of the legendary 'Barnum' coaches produced by the Great Central carriage works at Dukinfield, which was not very far from Ashbury. DE320709 entered traffic in 1910 as Open Third No 666. It became 5666, and in 1958 was transferred to departmental use and renumbered. Panelled stock was sometimes partially re-clad with planking in Departmental service. The 'Barnums' were built with matchboard sides. In GCR days they were fitted with J G Robinson's steel anti-collision fenders which were saw-tooth steel castings intended to prevent telescoping. Weighing as much as 37 tons each, the 'Barnums' were some of the heaviest eight-wheelers in the country at the time. DW320709 is in the Civil Engineers' black livery introduced at the formation of BR and which remained current until the start of the 1960s. It was photographed at Stamford in June 1966, when allocated to the Divisional Engineer, King's Cross, for use as a mobile workshop. It remained in BR use, latterly at Barnetby, until 1983. In GC days, the company heraldic device appeared on the frosted glass toilet windows, and there seems to be some traces of this on the near toilet window.

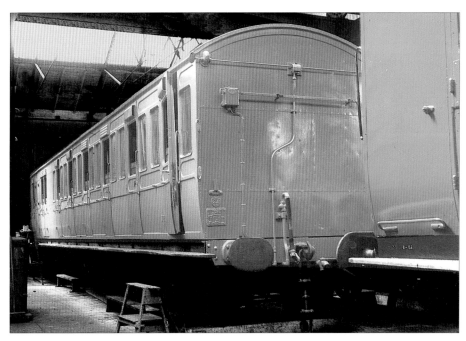

Top right: In 1912, the Lancing carriage works of the London Brighton & South Coast Railway produced three six-compartment Brake Thirds, Nos 851-853. During the grim days of the First World War, the railways came under government control, which was exercised by the Railway Executive Committee. Military needs were communicated to the REC, and the companies advised accordingly. To meet the shortage of munitions and weapons, much of the railway works capacity was switched to meeting military needs, but transport remained a vital national service, and a few coaches were turned out, including 15 more identical brake thirds in 1916. LBSCR No 852 became Southern Railway 4030, and was one of sixteen carriages to this design that were sent to the Isle of Wight. It became IoW section No 4156, and is seen in Ryde carriage works undergoing a major overhaul on 20th August 1963. To see a timber bodied pre-grouping coach receiving a major body overhaul at so late a date was exceptional. S4156 lasted until the demise of steam services on 31st December 1966. It was broken up in July 1967.

Bottom: Traditionally, BR departmental stock has provided a rich haul of elderly vehicles surviving long after they had become extinct in traffic, but in the north of England, the National Coal Board provided another refuge for some remarkable carriages. The leading coach in this rake at Ashington colliery is NCB 9300/163. This began life in 1913 as a Diagram 178 North Eastern Railway all Third No 118. It became LNER 2118, and was sold to the NCB in 1955. It was preserved in 1968. The 'Bath Men Only' inscription is so that men who have washed will not have to travel with colliers who have just come up from underground. The locomotive, NCB Northumberland area No 39, is a Robert Stephenson & Hawthorn 0-6-0T supplied in the 1950s. Instead of acquiring a Brake Third, Ashington colliery used an antiquated goods brake. One reason for selecting certain vehicles for this volume has been to show how much scope there is for unusual juxtapositions in real life. The combination of BR Mk I stock in blue and grey, and an NCB rake composed of entirely pre-group equipment is another attractive time warp for the modeller.

Top: On 8th June 1974, I was walking along the platform at Weybourne station on the North Norfolk Railway, and spotted a carriage bearing the Russian double-headed Imperial Eagle with orb and sceptre. The 'Russian Imperial Saloon', resplendent with no fewer than five double-headed eagles, had been used in a film and is seen here on a wedding special. It departs from Weybourne station in the mellow evening sunshine. The coach had been built at Wolverton as LNWR 5318 in 1913 to Diagram 2 as a Directors' Special Saloon. It was 66ft 6in long, and was carried on heavy six-wheel bogies. It became LMS 10500 in 1924 and 45002 under the 1933 renumbering scheme. It was taken out of service as BR M45002M, and preserved by the North Norfolk Railway in 1969.

Above: Under Thomas Clayton, the Midland Railway carriage superintendent from 1873, Derby gained a reputation for outstanding coaching stock. Clayton is best remembered for the clerestory stock he produced early in his career, and for an improved version in his later designs. So well established was the style, that when David Bain succeeded him in 1901, the clerestory was retained until 1913-14 when the modern high elliptical roof was adopted. MR 3463 was a 12-wheel restaurant car built to Diagram 575 at Derby in 1914, and one of the last clerestories built for the Midland Railway. Out of use by 1954, it was eventually preserved by the British Railways Board, and restored in 1957, It was on display at Clapham from 1963 to 1975, and then moved to the National Railway Museum at York.

Below: The whole of Ireland was still part of the United Kingdom during the First World War, and the railways of Ireland faced similar burdens to their mainland counterparts, often with far fewer resources. The Great Northern of Ireland connected Dublin and Belfast, and was hard pressed to cope with troop and other traffic, so was permitted to add a limited number of carriages to its fleet. GNR(I) 217, later UTA N206, was a solitary class O Brake First Third built in 1917, a second example, GNR No 64 being added three years later. Soon after the delivery of No 64, both were converted to class J4. Unlike the railways of mainland Britain, most of which had abolished Second class before World War 1, the Irish lines had retained the three classes, and the 'J' series were Tri-Composite Brakes. Including the two conversions, six J4s were built. No 217 was 58 foot long, with a 13 ft 10 in brake section and

seated 12 First, 12 Second and 21 Third class passengers. All were fitted for slipping. Under slip coach working, the carriage was fitted with a special slip coupling, and as an express approached a station at speed, a specially trained slip guard released the coupling and brake pipes whilst the train was in motion, and using a vacuum brake control in the coach slowed it to a standstill in the platform. This required great skill and judgment. Slipping permitted express trains to set down passengers at intermediate stations without stopping. This practice was popular in the early part of the last century. The last slip working in the British Isles was at Bicester on the Western Region of British Railways in 1960. Depending on condition, the UTA categorised the stock as A, B, C, or Scrap. No 217 was given B status, and is seen outside Adelaide shed on 21st August 1965.

Bottom: We have already visited Ashington Colliery, but No 9300/166 merits coverage. In 1919-1921, in the last years of its independent life, the Furness Railway, which ran from Carnforth (where it joined the West Coast Main Line) to Barrow and up the Cumbrian coast, added a number of nine-compartment Thirds to its stock. No 9300/166 started life as FR146 or 147, became LMS 15146/7, and under the 1933 renumbering scheme, became 15326/7, prior to being sold for colliery use. This illustration at Ashington in April 1968 recaptures the lines of these impressive late pre-grouping coaches excellently, and shows the design of bogie adopted by the Furness at this time.

Left: Few contemporary views of GWR brown
stock livery exist, so I have selected this
example of milk brake No 1399 to portray
another aspect of non-passenger coaching
stock, the milk train. This vehicle was built
during the First World War for use as pharmacy
car in one of the ambulance trains that had
been built for service in Britain or France to
transport wounded soldiers. In 1921 it was
converted into a milk brake, and transferred to
departmental duties in 1961. It was preserved
on the Severn Valley Railway in 1967, and is
seen at Bridgnorth in 1974. From the mid-
nineteenth century, the fast conveyance of milk
became ever more important as the cities of
Britain grew in size. Trains of churns, and later
tank wagons, moved milk at express passenger
speeds from the country districts to the main
towns and cities. This traffic continued in some
places until the 1970s when it succumbed to
road competition.

Below: David Bain of the Midland Railway
introduced the high elliptical roof 1915, and his
successor R W Reid improved the design. In
1922, Reid introduced a new 57 foot long
chassis with channel iron solebars and angle
iron trussing, rather than the round bar trussing
of earlier designs. Fourteen Corridor
Composite coaches to diagram D1281 were
turned out under Lot 971 in 1922-23. As well as
the use of heavier trussing, the 1922 stock
introduced tongue and groove boarded ends to
the Midland. They were superb vehicles, and
were to be highly influential, as the angle
trussed frame, high profile roof, and match
boarded ends set the pattern for the LMS
standard period I coach. In 1903, the Midland
Railway had taken over the Belfast & Northern
Counties Railway in Ireland, renaming it the
Midland Railway (Northern Counties
Committee). This became the LMS NCC in
1923. During the Second World War many NCC
carriages were destroyed in heavy air raids on
Belfast in 1941. To make good the deficiency,
the LMS sent four of the Diagram 1281
composites to Northern Ireland. LMS 4913
became NCC 65, and later UTA 272. It became
NCC class F3, and is depicted in service at York
Road station on 24th August 1966. The nearest
and fourth compartments are half
compartments, or coupes, a feature of Midland
design at this time.

1923-1947
THE YEARS OF CHANGE

Before the First World War, parliament had seen competition as the way to achieve good railway services, and mergers had been blocked. By 1918, the parliamentary mood had changed, and the main line railways in Great Britain were forcibly merged into four groups whether they liked it or not. This took place on 1st January 1923, and created four major companies. The Southern Railway, the London Midland & Scottish Railway and the London & North Eastern Railway were completely new organisations, whilst the fourth company, the Great Western, was an enlargement of the old GWR. In the interval between 1918 and 1923, southern Ireland had been granted independence, but six counties in the north opted to remain part of the United Kingdom. Railways operating exclusively in the south were merged into the Great Southern Railways in 1925, but the cross-border or Northern Ireland companies retained their separate identities. By 1922, steel underframes were normal for new construction, but bodywork was still timber. Fully beaded panelling was customary, as was an elaborately lined out livery. By the 1930s, three of the 'Big Four' had switched to steel bodies, beading was largely suppressed, and simplified liveries were being adopted.

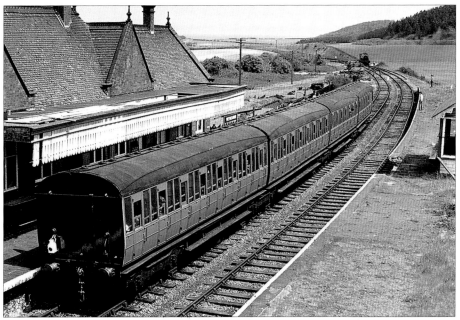

Top right: In the early months of the grouping, the carriage works of the 'Big Four' continued to build existing designs. Always referred to as a Brighton coach, Isle of Wight section 6349 was one of ten First/Third composites of LBSCR design built at Lancing in 1924, nine of which were sent to the island in 1936-37. Allocated the Brighton number 7, it almost certainly entered traffic as SR 6164, receiving its island number when transferred in April 1937. It was withdrawn in October 1966, and preserved by the IoW steam railway and is seen at Haven Street station some thirty years later. By this time it had been in preservation longer than it had been in commercial service on the island. Primarily operated by 'Terrier' tanks and the sole surviving Adams O2 tank, with matching period coaching stock, the IWSR is outstanding amongst preserved lines for its success in recapturing the image of yesteryear.

Above right: Nigel Gresley became carriage and wagon superintendent of the Great Northern Railway in 1905 and locomotive superintendent six years later. He was to stamp his personality on the East Coast main line for the rest of the steam era, with superb steam locomotives and elegant teak bodied coaching stock, some of which was still in use at the start of the 1970s. One of his most cherished ideas was articulation, in which two adjacent coaches share a common bogie. This offered significant savings in tare weight per passenger. Two six

wheelers were rebuilt as an articulated set in 1907, and by the 1920s the principle was well established, with triple, quad and quint-art sets. Examples of express and suburban stock had appeared in GN days, but the articulated principle is best remembered due to the legendary quad-art sets. Some twins were converted into quad-art sets in 1921-22 for suburban services out of King's Cross, and more sets were added in LNER days. Eventually there were 97 quad sets. Most stayed in the King's Cross area, but a few migrated elsewhere. The first replacement DMUs arrived in 1959, and the last quad-art was withdrawn in 1966. One set, No 74, comprising a Brake Third, a Third and two Composites. was preserved by the North Norfolk Railway in 1967. It is seen at Weybourne on 9th June 1974. The individual vehicles were to Diagrams 68B, 69, 70, and 71.

Right: The interior of the quad-arts was plain but adequate for commuters, and the sets were popular with travellers, as their high seating capacity gave a better chance of a seat than on the replacement DMUs or the BR Mk I suburban

stock which was also drafted in to eliminate the elderly quad-arts by 1966. Commuters preferred a more basic coach with a seat to the joys of standing in a more modern vehicle!

Left: When the LMS came into existence in 1923, it inherited Midland and LNWR traditions. Given the preponderance of Midland men in high office on the LMS, Derby ideas predominated, creating the LMS Period 1 coach. It was a fully beaded wooden bodied coach with matchboard ends, and the body and chassis were a copy of late MR practice. Period 2, from about 1929 to 1932, saw a lower waist and window level, the use of larger picture windows, and a move towards reduced beading and the wider use of steel panelling. Period 3 witnessed the emergence of the flush-sided Stanier steel stock with rounded corners to the windows. In 1923, the LMS received an urgent request from its Irish subsidiary, now the LMS NCC. The Northern Counties was worried about its archaic stock, but York Road works could not cope, and Derby was asked to supply 30 bogie carriages, including a dining saloon. Because the LMS had many 12 wheel 65 or 68 foot diners from the LNWR and MR, it had no suitable dining car design. However the Midland Third Open had become an LMS standard. As this had a centre aisle with large tables, it was suitable as a dining saloon. NCC class B3 Third class dining saloon No 89, later UTA No 162, was delivered in 1924. It seated 56 passengers in two large saloons. It closely followed LMS Diagram D1353 and was 9ft 6in wide. Each seating bay was provided with two windows, one fixed and one droplight. There was a Stones' pattern ventilator in the eaves panel above each of the fixed lights. It has lost some of the Stone's ventilators, but other than that, had hardly altered in more than 40 years when photographed at the carriage sidings at York Road station, Belfast on 27th August 1967.

Centre: In the 1870s, the Festiniog and Isle of Man Railways had been at the cutting edge of technology, introducing bogie stock at a time when the main line companies preferred four-wheel or six-wheel designs. By the mid 1920s, the narrow gauge was feeling the winds of adversity, and when the Metropolitan Carriage Wagon & Finance Co delivered F49 to the IMR in 1926, it was to mark the end of a 50 year association. The Isle of Man Railway Company would never order another carriage. F49 was a Third/Brake of a type developed for the IOMR in the late 1890s. It was the first IMR coach to be delivered new with vacuum brakes, for the IMR was not covered by the UK Regulation of Railway Act of 1889, so was not statutorily obliged to have continuous automatic brakes on its passenger trains. F49 is seen in red and cream livery at Douglas on 29 May 1967. The LMS NCC was to acquire some magnificent narrow gauge corridor coaches and the GWR was to re-equip the Vale of Rheidol Railway in the 1930s, but after that no further narrow gauge coaches were to appear until the preservation era.

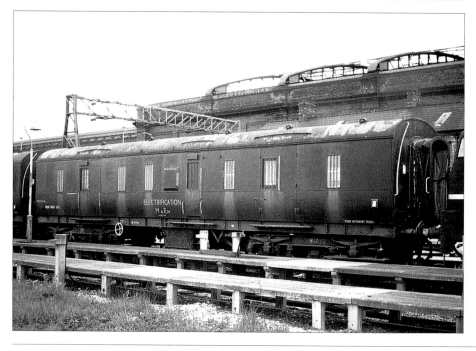

Opposite page, bottom: Weathered Engineers Department black had done nothing for the appearance of former LMS BG DM395665, once M30617M. Even so, when I first saw it, I thought there was something odd about it, but it was some time before I discovered what it was. Unlike standard LMS BGs, it does not have the normal angle iron trussing. It does not need it, for it is an integral construction all steel brake to diagram D1715. Between 1926 and 1930, 360 of these vans were supplied to the LMS, and 30617 was one of a batch of fifty built by the Metropolitan Carriage, Wagon & Finance Co in 1927. Despite its all-metal build, the body style was identical to conventional Period 1 LMS BGs. They were withdrawn between 1958 and 1966. A few, including DM395665, recorded at Rugby on 11th May 1972 as a mobile instrument store, survived in departmental use. It would have housed calibrating equipment for tensioning the overhead 25kv line. Locomotive buffs may recognise the vehicle to the right of the picture. It is former GWR Gas Turbine 18100, later rebuilt as E2001.

Top: M255M was another important LMS Period 1 vehicle. It began life in 1928 as LMS 504 when the company introduced Third class sleeping cars. Eighty-five Period 1 cars were built to Diagram D1709 in 1928-31. They were the first vehicles on a new 60-foot underframe, and only 15 more Stanier-type Third class sleepers were built by the LMS before nationalisation. During the Second World War, many of the Third sleepers were converted to ambulance coaches, some of which were rebuilt after the war into cafeteria cars. No 504 became a Diagram 2195 cafeteria car with a new number, M255M, in the LMS dining car series. The rebuild was carried out at Eastleigh, and blended LMS Period 1 and 2, and maybe even a dash of Maunsell in the overall design! In the introduction, I spoke of going 'Duchess hunting' and coming home with a bag of coaching stock ex-Wolverton works. This was the 'crown jewels' of that selection, on a lovely sunny 30th July 1964. The body is in good condition but not ex-works, however the windows are gleaming and the interior seems to be pristine, so it is likely that M255M had just received an interior refurbishment. The entire class went between December 1964 and November 1965.

Above: For many years, there were two stations at Peterborough; the well-known GNR station on the East Coast Main line, and the more obscure GER Peterborough East station, used by the GE itself and by the LNWR. E. L. Ahrons, writing in 1918, said of Peterborough East that the station appeared not to have been touched up since a visit by the King of Mercia in 655AD. When my father and I visited the station, we sympathised with Ahrons' observations, but we did chance upon this splendid Gresley TPO, so all was forgiven. E70279E, originally LNER 2339, was one of three Diagram D131 TPOs ordered under the 1927/28 carriage building programme, but not delivered until 1929. They were the first TPOs built by the LNER after the grouping and were put on the King's Cross to Newcastle service. In 1932, they were transferred to the GE section for the Liverpool Street to Peterborough run, where they remained until 1966-67. The body was only 8 feet wide at floor level, but was built out on the non-net side to accommodate sorting racks over most of the body length. E70279E was photographed at Peterborough East on 1st June 1966.

Left: Dw150342, seen at Banbury on 13th June 1965, recalls a cherished Great Western institution, the auto coach. A dozen coaches, including No 160 were built to Diagram A27 in 1928-29, and their lines recaptured the looks of the pre-war GWR steam railcars, some of which were still running at the time. Indeed, some steam railcar bodies were converted to auto coaches. No 160 survived in service until 1962 when it was transferred to departmental duties. It was acquired by the Severn Valley in 1969 as a source of spares and broken up later that same year. Fortunately other diagram A27 auto coaches have been preserved.

Opposite page, centre: Few good pre-war colour views exist of locomotives, let alone of coaching stock, so it is a pleasure to include this unpublished Dufaycolor slide from 1935. It is taken at Leamington Spa, and shows an up Aberystwyth to Paddington express departing from Leamington. The nearer coach, No 6012, is a 56-foot Collett Diagram E132 composite built in 1928, with 4 First and 3 Third class compartments. The coach is in the 'shirt button' livery, which had only been introduced in September 1934. First class compartments are still lettered, but lettering of Third class compartments had ceased about 1930, so they are unmarked. Individual doors were still provided to each compartment, and also on the gangway side. The bodywork is clean, but the white roof has weathered to a medium grey in less than a year, whilst the bogies and underframe detail are decidedly grimy. This is what GWR coaches were like in everyday service. Glossy white roofs and gloss black underframes may look pretty on a model, but they did not stay like that for long. The leading coach is a Collett Diagram D95 Brake Third. Two batches were built, 4913-44 in 1927 and 5087-5132 in 1928. In 1927, the GWR abolished all lining on passenger stock, and abandoned the old garter device in favour of the arms of London and Bristol in 1928. In 1930, the company relented, and reintroduced gold and black waist lining for stock on important services, so this carriage has received a repaint into 1930-34 livery. *H J Stretton Ward*

Opposite page, bottom: 1930s colour film was very slow, with speeds of 6-10ASA. Today, 100 ASA is regarded as a slow film, and 200 or 400 ASA is normal. With such slow film speed, action photography was difficult, and most pre-war colour views show engines at rest, rather than an express in full cry. This portrait of a Southern express is one of the few pre-war action shots of a Maunsell express in all its glory. It was taken at 1/100th second at F4.5. It depicts No 772 *Sir Percivale*, a Maunsell 'King Arthur' class 4-6-0 approaching Hewish Summit, west of Crewkerne at about midday, with what is thought to be the 8.45am ex Waterloo, on Saturday 13th August 1938. The leading two carriages are Diagram 2005 Open Thirds, the first twenty of which were authorised in April 1929 (Nos 1369-1388), and completed in 1930. Further batches followed to the same design. The Diagram 2005 Open Thirds were often used as strengthening vehicles or trailers to kitchen cars on the West of England expresses. The bodies were 9 ft wide with recessed doors at the ends. In earlier designs, it was common for the windows in the doors to be openable, hence the term droplight, but the large picture windows that were becoming common in the 1930s were ordinarily fixed. The large windows on the open thirds could be lowered 7 inches to provide ventilation. Both features are clearly visible in this view. The Maunsell locomotive and coach livery is captured very well in this rare pre-war scene. The Open Thirds were withdrawn between 1959 and 1964.

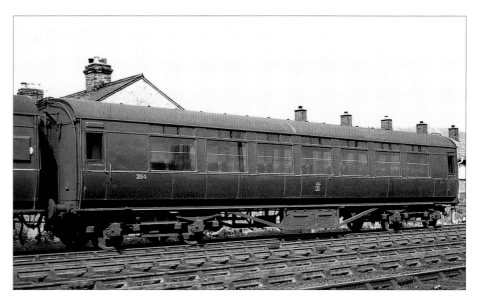

This page, top: In the 1930s the LMS NCC decided to introduce a luxury train for the long distance commuter traffic between Belfast and the seaside resort of Portrush on the north coast. Though Stanier had recently been appointed Chief mechanical Engineer of the LMS, he was happy to leave the NCC to its own devices. York Road's adoption of five foot long picture windows and the elimination of the waist panel gave the new 'North Atlantic Express' stock a superficial similarity to LMS Period 2 designs. My impression is that the York Road drawing office had spoken to their counterparts at Derby and studied plans of Period 2 stock and then improved the design for their new train. Five carriages were built, Nos 90-92 in 1934 and Nos 93 and 94 in 1935. The final coach was No 94, a J8 class Corridor Third, with seven compartments which seated just 42 passengers. The interior was in polished mahogany with Venetian bronze fittings. Instead of prints or photographs in the compartments, coloured original etchings by the artist Creswell Boak, added distinction. These survived until the Second World war when large numbers of US servicemen were stationed in Ulster. NCC men always said that most of the prints found their way across the Atlantic during these years. No 94 later became UTA No 394 and is seen here at York Road on 26th August 1966.

Above: Mail trains had run for the Post Office from the dawn of the railway age, but underwent a marked improvement in the 1930s. M30230M, seen at Manchester Victoria in April 1968, is a POS, or Post Office Sorting van, to Diagram D 1792. This Diagram covered 27 vehicles, an exceptionally large class for TPOs, built from 1930 to 1939, and was the definitive LMS sorting van. The first 13 were to Period 2 design, and the rest, including 30230, which came from Wolverton under Lot 987 in 1936, to Period 3. Some were built without pick-up nets, and others lost them later. Some had toilets; others did not, but all were fitted with the late posting letterbox, painted in Post Office red. In the 1930s, when my father was stationed at Millbank in London, he could post a letter to my mother first thing in the morning. She would receive it about midday at the hospital in Liverpool where she was working. If she replied by about 1.00pm, my father could receive the reply in the last evening delivery about 6.30pm. With the improved first class service of today, the cost has increased 44-fold, and instead of 12-14 hours, it would take at least three days from posting a letter to receiving the reply. This is called progress! For modellers, the Victorian skyline in the heart of a big city is a reminder of what life was like at end of the steam age.

Left: The LMS had adopted flush sided steel bodied stock, but on the LNER, Nigel Gresley stuck to the elegant teak coaches he had developed in 1906, only a few months after he became Carriage & Wagon Superintendent of the GNR. The LNER workshops were still equipped to produce wooden bodies, and as they were robust and long-lived, Gresley saw no reason to abandon a sound design. In the early 1930s, the existing restaurant cars were complemented by the construction of buffet cars for use on services that did not merit a full restaurant car. Diagram 167 was introduced in 1933. E9124E was one of 15 Diagram 167 buffet cars to emerge from York carriage shops in 1937. They were 61ft 6in long, and outlasted the LNER by many years. By the time I photographed E9124E at Manchester Piccadilly in a rake of BR Mk Is on 27th April 1971, it carried corporate blue and grey colours, with a red catering stock band. Gresley died on the 5th April 1941, but I am sure that the survival of some of his passenger stock for more than 30 years after his death would have pleased him.

Centre left: The Gresley bogie brake van appeared in 1906, and similar vehicles were produced until 1943. Thirty years on, they were still plentiful. They shared the same domed ends to the roof and panelling of the passenger stock, and provide modellers with an opportunity to operate modern traction alongside fully panelled coaching stock without compromising accuracy. There were several standard designs. All were 61ft 6in x 9ft over the body. There were teak or steel bodied vehicles. Some had duckets; some did not. Some had welded underframes, others had riveted frames. There were also non-standard variants, such as the short GE section vans. E70473E is a 61ft 6in Diagram 245 pigeon van, and was one of five vehicles ordered under the 1937 carriage building programme, but not actually built at York until 1939. Pigeon racing was very popular, especially in the north of Britain, and every week tens of thousands of pigeons were dispatched by rail many hundreds of miles. The racing pigeon associations were important customers with friends in high places, and as many owners accompanied their pigeons to the release point, they were able to insist on electrically lit corridor vans. The pigeons were conveyed in wicker baskets carried on shelving along the van sides. They were stacked in the yard at the release point and railway staff and owners would release them at the correct time, so that a cloud of pigeons rose into the air, circled for a while to get their bearings, and then flew to their home lofts. E70473E was in weathered rail blue when photographed passing through Rugby on 1st July 1971. At this time, parcels stock received destination labels that were much bigger than the standard wagon label. The BG to the left of the picture has a parcels label clip.

Bottom left: The Great Western Siphon G was another long-lived design. The word Siphon comes from the telegraphic reporting code, and the first four wheel or six wheel siphons were for milk or fish traffic. Bogie versions followed, but rather than being confined to milk trains, the Siphon was an all purpose bogie van for everything from theatrical scenery and Christmas parcels to newspapers and pigeons. The Siphon G was plentiful, but the telegraph code name does not relate to just one diagram, but to a generic type. Some of the first Siphon Gs appeared to Diagram 0.11 in 1913. They were outside framed, and construction continued until 1927. An inside framed version, Diagram 0.22 appeared in 1926-29, quickly followed by another very similar design 0.33, issued in July 1930. Further designs appeared into the 1950s. Although notionally milk vans, milk was increasingly conveyed by rail tankers in the 1930s, and many Siphons spent most of their time carrying parcels, luggage and even pigeons. W2917W, seen at Wisbech on 1st October 1972, was the first Diagram 0.33 Siphon G built to Lot 1651 in 1940. It is in weathered rail blue, but what is particularly useful is that the doors are open, showing the interior paint scheme, and the two rows of folding shelves that made the Siphon such a versatile vehicle.

Top right: Unlike the Siphon G, which continued to be built because of its versatility, the horsebox was highly specialised, and as horses were eclipsed by the motor vehicle, the demand for horseboxes declined. Nevertheless a few horseboxes were built to replace time expired stock. At the start of the previous section we illustrated a grounded GWR Diagram N9 horsebox of c1900. UTA N635 looks even more venerable, but was built as GNR(I) No 618 at Dundalk in 1940. It is to the usual style, with a groom's compartment with a door and a droplight window at the right hand end. The central horse compartment has a lower drop door and two upper cupboard doors, and there is a provender compartment at the near end. Movable partitions allow the box to carry 1, 2 or

3 horses. The springing is very crude for such a late period vehicle.

Above: The LMS integral construction steel BG appeared earlier in this section. It is time to look at the standard LMS 50-foot BG. Although several diagrams existed, differences were trivial. M31195 has lost the suffix that denotes pre-nationalisation origin, but displays all the design features of the Period 3 BG. Diagram D2007 appeared in 1938, 31195 being built at Wolverton in 1941 as a part of Lot 1305. Almost 400 Diagram 2007 vans were built, most of which were still active at the start of the 1970s. The ribbed steel Stanier roof is particularly clear in this view. By the time M31195 was photographed at Gloucester on 1st July 1976, it

had lost its end gangways and the aperture had been plated over, converting it to a B. This modification was applied to many Diagram 2007 BGs, and is one of many ways that a modeller can customise his stock. On steel stock, corrosion of the body panels just above floor level was a serious problem, and this vehicle has considerable re-plating. This is another way that rolling stock can be customised. Finally there is the weathering pattern. Road dirt is particularly heavy on the ends and on the sides below waist level. The chalked inscriptions complete the image of a working vehicle, and if reproduced in model form, will make an immense difference to authenticity.

One paradox of Second World War era was that although ordinary coach construction virtually ceased, the LMS and the GWR built several special saloons. The LMS created two Chairman's saloons, and the GWR constructed a pair of equally luxurious saloons. All four were built on the chassis of coaches destroyed through enemy action. GWR 9006 was built to Diagram G64 on the chassis of a 1938 Corridor Third. Construction was protracted, and 9006 was not completed until 1945. It had a small kitchen and staff sleeping accommodation at one end, an eight seat dining saloon, a bathroom, two state bedrooms and an observation saloon/lounge at the other end. By 1948, 9006 (and a similar saloon No 9007) had been refurbished for use on the GWR royal train. It carried Great Western chocolate and cream colours for many years, and it was only after the WR royal train was disbanded, that the two special saloons received the LM Region royal train purple lake livery. No 9006 was withdrawn in 1984, and after a spell on display at the NRM, was put into the reserve collection, and stored under high security conditions at the Ministry of Defence depot at Kineton.

The lounge was provided with four loose armchairs, a settee for three, and a pair of coffee tables. The corridor connection was entered directly off the saloon, and was flanked by generous observation windows. The purpose of these two saloons has always been shrouded in secrecy, but there is reason to believe that the conversion of a pair of bomb damaged Collett coaches to special saloons may have been to provide a mobile command centre for Winston Churchill during his many wartime journeys touring military establishments and raising morale.

A short side corridor ran from the lounge to the dining saloon, with a further corridor running past the staff accommodation and kitchen. Given the protracted building period for both saloons, it is a moot point how much use Churchill made of them. Later, with further upgrading, they were used by the royal family on Western Region journeys.

Below: With the expansion of electric services, steam hauled stock customarily took a back seat in the Southern stock building programmes, and the last Maunsell carriages were built in 1936. His successor O V S Bulleid took over in 1937. Before any new passenger carriages could be built, war broke out, and it was not until 1945-46 that the prototype Bulleid coaching stock appeared. Several hundred Bulleid coaches were turned out over the next few years, construction continuing into BR days, and they remained in first line service into the 1960s. In this study of 'Merchant Navy' pacific No 35030 *Elder Dempster Lines*, powering through Brockenhurst with the down 'Royal Wessex' on 12th June 1965, Bulleid stock predominates. The leading vehicle is a semi-open Brake Third built for the Bournemouth line services in 1947-48. The set number, 298, is painted prominently on the end of the outer vehicle of each diagrammed set. The use of Bulleid stock on one of the prestige services from Waterloo shows how highly the Bulleid stock was valued by the Southern Region.

Bottom: Although the railways of mainland Britain had been affected by rising costs and road competition, the plight of the Irish railways was far worse. Even the prestigious GNR(I) found it hard to cover its costs. In 1933, the GN civil engineer, George B Howden was appointed Mechanical Engineer, and two years later, Dundalk built its first steel bodied passenger stock. These were the celebrated K15 all thirds, and the F16 composites. Instead of traditional panelled bodies, flush-sided steel bodies were adopted, with semi-open interiors and modern tubular frame seats. More coaches came at regular intervals into the war years. They were turned out in imitation varnished wood, akin to the LNER experiments with simulated wood finish on steel stock. During the war, to cope with the the extra passenger numbers on offer,, the GN built a batch of carriages with K15 body shells, but instead of the 70 seats of the K15, the new workmen's coaches seated from 98 to 108 passengers. They became class K23. After the war they were

rebuilt as 70 seaters, becoming class K15. GNR No 176, later UTA N583, was refurbished in 1947. The tubular steel seat frames are clearly visible in this portrait at Great Victoria St station, Belfast on 26th August 1966. In 1958, the assets of the railway were equally divided between the Ulster Transport Authority in the north and the Coras Iompair Eireann in the south, and the GN liveries, varnished wood for steam stock, and blue and cream for railcars, started to disappear. Seven years later, the UTA decided its dark green livery was too sombre, and adopted regional colours, reintroducing blue and cream, but adopting a much livelier shade of blue, and a very pale ivory. It was an eye-catching livery, but by 1970, the newly formed Northern Ireland Railways adopted a system-wide red and ivory-white colour scheme. The corridor connections on No 176 show that it had been rebuilt to run with the GNR(I) BUT diesel railcar sets, which had the continental-style tubular rubber roll connections.

Above: On the LNER, Sir Nigel Gresley had died in office in April 1941. His successor, Edward Thompson, was another engineer in a hurry, with much that he wanted to do, and little time left before his retirement. New steel bodied prototypes were built in 1944-45 with longer and deeper windows than with the Gresley designs. Although the GWR was adopting the bowed end to the roof, Thompson went the other way, adopting a straight profile. Gresley had built a few bodies with steel cladding on a wooden framework, but this became the standard pattern after 1944. After Thompson's retirement in 1946, Arthur Peppercorn took over, and made a few detail improvements. The most obvious was the use of rounded corners to the windows from 1949, as the square cornered windows on metal bodies suffered from corrosion. DE321134, which is seen after transfer to the CCE as a mess van, began life as E13868E, and was an all Third built to Diagram 329 at York in 1949. It displays the Peppercorn window, Thompson body and the traditional Gresley bogie. It was transferred to the LM Region, and later carried the olive green livery adopted for CCE stock in the early 1960s.

Top: C B Collett, who had succeeded G J Churchward as CME of the GWR, retired in 1941, after almost twenty years in office. His successor was F W Hawksworth. Coming to office in time of war, with the post-war austerity years and nationalisation to follow, Hawksworth's freedom of action was limited, but he made several improvements in motive power, and created some of the most elegant steel bodied stock ever built. Longer panoramic windows were fitted to corridor stock, and the roof was domed in Gresley fashion at the ends. Construction of Hawksworth stock continued for some time after nationalisation, and W7372W, built under Lot 1690 at Swindon to Diagram E164, did not appear until 1948. It was a Corridor Brake Composite, and along with W7277W, was used as a part of the Western Region royal train. As with the special saloons illustrated earlier, it received chocolate and cream, the WR royal train livery. Unlike the saloons, it did not go into the LM royal train, but was put back into ordinary service. Seen here in September 1967, it later went to the Great Western Society at Didcot. The GWR corridor connection and its support arms and the shell roof ventilators show to perfection.

Right: On the LMS there had also been a change of chief. Sir William Stanier had been seconded for government service, and then succeeded by C E Fairburn, who died after only a few moths in office. His successor was H G Ivatt. The final developments in LMS coaching stock, the so called 'porthole' stock, with circular toilet windows, different ventilators and other minor changes, did not appear until after nationalisation, but were pure LMS in concept. M24603M was one of seventy-five Corridor Composites (CK) built to Diagram D2159 under Lot 1500 at Derby in 1949-50. It is on a through North East to South West working, and has a Newcastle label on the near window. In common with many of the early steel panelled designs, it has suffered corrosion where the panel joins the flooring, and has been plated throughout the entire length of the bodywork. It carries BR maroon livery, which appeared in two variants, with black or with maroon ends. By the time this view was taken in 1967, LMS passenger stock in service was becoming a rarity.

Below: The final company designed sleeping cars appeared after the demise of the 'Big Four'. On the Eastern Region, Doncaster built five 66ft 6in pressure-ventilated First class sleepers to Diagram 359 in 1950. As with the Peppercorn CK, these received rounded corners to the windows to minimise corrosion. At the time these vehicles were built, asbestos cladding between the outer and inner body shells was regarded as perfectly safe. E1259E was withdrawn and sold to the North Yorkshire Moors Railway in 1968. It is seen in June 1969 shortly after its arrival at Grosmont. It is still in ex BR condition, without any alterations to livery, lettering or bodywork, so provides a valuable guide to Eastern Region livery practice. By the 1980s, asbestos was thought to be as much of a threat to the human species as nuclear war, and asbestos removal had to be carried out by specialist contractors with all the right equipment. Asbestos removal began in 1988, but something went badly wrong and E1259E caught fire and was burnt out. The coach had to be broken up. It was the sole surviving diagram D359 sleeper, and the type is now extinct.

Top: The last LMS First class sleepers were built to Diagram 2166, and appeared from Wolverton in 1951-52. They were a post-war development of the 1935-36 Diagram 1926 sleeper. At 69 feet, they were even longer than the LNER sleepers, and were carried on two six-wheel bogies. At 47 tons each, they were amongst the heaviest steam age passenger stock ever built. They entered service in BR carmine and cream, then became maroon and many received corporate blue and grey. M398M, one of five cars built under Lot 1570 in 1951, is seen at Wolverton works in January 1969. Points of interest include the recessed door handles, the roof ducting for the pressure ventilation system, and the usual patching of the bodywork just above solebar level. They were withdrawn between August 1966 and the mid-1970s. No fewer than seven of the 25 Diagram 2166 SLFs were preserved, M398M going to the Bluebell Railway after a spell in departmental service as DB975188. The reason why sleeping cars have a surprisingly high survival rate has been that prior to the privatisation of BR, they were useful as staff accommodation coaches on civil engineering projects, and they have also provided useful accommodation for volunteers on the preserved railways.

Above: In this section on grouping era stock, it is ironic but appropriate that the our concluding vehicle is one of the last of pre-nationalisation design built by BR, though ironically, its design predated the grouping companies. The first of the Maunsell four-wheel passenger luggage vans appeared on the SE&CR as long ago as 1919. In 1925, Maunsell proposed a 'utility van' (or Van U) with side and end doors. It could be used for parcels, or as a covered carriage truck; it could convey light field guns, small aeroplanes, fruit or milk, and would replace the myriad of different vehicles that had hitherto been needed. Re-designated CCT or Covered Carriage Truck by BR, a name that did not reflect its general utility role as well as the Southern title, a final order, L3764, for 50 CCTs, to be numbered 2501-2550, was placed with Lancing Carriage works in 1955. S2517 was built in August 1955, the final deliveries coming shortly before Christmas. As an economy measure, the van sides were plywood rather than planked as with the Southern examples. S2517 is seen at Gloucester on 1st July 1976. It was withdrawn in 1981, and the last examples were taken out of revenue service five years later. Several have been preserved.

1948-1960
NEW NAMES, NEW DESIGNS

By 1945, the 'Big Four' grouped companies in mainland Britain had become familiar names. In the Irish Free State, the Great Southern Railways had also been around for 20 years, and the Great Northern Railway (Ireland) was celebrating its 70th birthday. In little more than a decade, all these famous names were to vanish. First to go was the GSR, merged with Dublin United Transport Company in 1945 to form Coras Iompair Eireann. Initially a private company with Irish Government support, it was nationalised in 1950. In 1945, a Labour government came to power in the United Kingdom. Dedicated to nationalising all important industries, transport was on the hit list, and despite strong opposition from the 'Big Four', the government majority in parliament ensured that the opinions of professional railway officers counted for nothing. The 1947 Transport Act set up the British Transport Commission, which was to exercise control over all forms of public transport through its 'Executives'. The Railway Executive would run the publicly owned railways under the title British Railways from 1st January 1948.

The lines operating solely within Northern Ireland passed to a similar body, the Ulster Transport Authority, from 1st April 1948, the LMS NCC being run for three months by 'the Railway Executive-NCC'. By the end of 1950, other than for a few light railways, such as the Talyllyn or the Londonderry & Lough Swilly, the only trunk line left bearing its traditional name was the Great Northern Railway (Ireland). The GN faced formidable financial problems, and in 1953, the Belfast and Dublin governments took over the bankrupt concern under the title Great Northern Railway Board, each government appointing representatives. In 1958, the board was abolished, and its remaining lines and assets were divided equally between the two governments and the last of the powerful companies of yesteryear faded into history.

In this part of the book, following these changes, we will see how locomotive hauled stock evolved between 1948 and 1960.

Below: One of the proclaimed benefits of nationalisation was the possibility of standardised equipment that could operate anywhere. Design, building, operating and repair costs would benefit from the economies of scale, and the newly formed Railway Executive agreed that developing a range of standard coaches was a priority, given the run down state of many carriages due to age or wartime neglect. A new Carriage Standards Committee set out the parameters. To provide good route availability, the maximum acceptable length for gangwayed stock was to be 63ft 6in. The width could be 8ft 8½ins if the body profile was slightly altered and guard's projecting lookouts or duckets were abandoned. Although integral construction, in which there is no separate chassis, offered theoretical benefits, the convenience of a separate chassis had other advantages, not least flexibility in body design. Whilst steel panelling became prevalent in the 1930s, it was usually secured to a wooden framework, but after the war, good quality wood and skilled woodworkers were in short supply, so the new body was to be steel clad and attached to steel frames. Pre-nationalisation stock had an end load resistance of between 80 and 120 tons in the event of collision. The Standards Committee laid down a figure of 200 tons. Construction was to be by jigs, to ensure maximum standardisation. The prototype Mark I coach appeared in September 1950, with early production examples emerging six months later. It was to become one of the most successful and numerous families of passenger stock to have entered service anywhere in the world. W34880 and W34772 are a pair of Mk Is built to Diagram 182. W34772 was one of sixty Corridor Brake Thirds built under Lot 30157 at Wolverton in 1955, whilst W34880 was one of twelve vehicles built by Charles Roberts to Lot 30223 in 1956. Both are in carmine and cream in this 1957 study at Leamington Spa. The third vehicle is a Diagram 171 or 172 Corridor Brake Composite. It is wintertime, and the steam heating system is in use. The reporting code for a Corridor Brake Third was BTK, or after Third class was re-designated Second class, a BSK.

Top: The Mk I was not a single type of carriage, but a range of stock, mounted on standard chassis, and built to standard body profiles with uniform window sizes. W1732, a diagram 24 restaurant buffet car, seen at Leamington Spa on 3rd July 1964, was built to Lot 30512 by the Birmingham Railway Carriage & Wagon Company in 1961. To improve the riding qualities of this heavy vehicle, BR2 bogies are fitted, as indicated by the BR2 lettering on the axlebox covers. Vibration damping units are also fitted to the spring hangers. In the early years of BR, when all decisions were taken at headquarters, gangwayed stock was painted in carmine and cream regardless of regional allocation. A more decentralised system was set up in 1956, which allowed the regions some say in their liveries. Predictably the Western Region resurrected GWR chocolate and cream for its

prestige services, whilst the Southern selected green. The LM region opted for LMS maroon, but when there were rumours that the Eastern and North Eastern Regions wanted to reintroduce grained teak on steel bodied stock, BR headquarters put its foot down, and decreed maroon for the rest of the system. Because the pre-nationalisation catering cars were in better condition than most stock, the initial requirement for catering vehicles was limited, and it was not until the second wave of Mk I building from 1957 onwards that large numbers of catering cars appeared. The Buffet-Restaurant Car (coded RB) was a midway stage between a full restaurant car and the more limited resources of a buffet car, as social habits were changing, and there was a growing demand for light snacks as compared to the multiple course dining car meal. It was expected that passengers

would board the train to find a seat, go to the RB for a meal, and then return to their seat. To make best use of space, the RB received few external doors, but for safety reasons, emergency doors were provided in the seating and kitchen areas. They were distinguished by no glazing or external handles, an internal glass panel had to be smashed in order to open the door from inside. The near door on W1732 is such an emergency exit.

Left: The Griddle Car was an unusual vehicle, and initially just three were built, the chassis coming from Ashford, and the bodies from Eastleigh. Nos 1100-1102 were built to Diagram 30 under Lot 30637 in 1960, one each going to the Scottish, Western and London Midland regions for evaluation. The idea was to provide a car with a two or three man crew that could provide a range of drinks and hot food from a griddle plate. Sc1100 appeared on a morning Inverness-Edinburgh working, and afternoon return service. Unlike many restaurant cars, where the kitchen was at one end, here it was in the centre, with a buffet saloon at the near end and a bar saloon at the far end. This is the kitchen side of SC1100, and once again there is an emergency door just to the left of the 'Griddle' inscription. On withdrawal, SC1100 was restored to maroon livery and included in the Travellers Fare commemorative special in 1979. It is seen on this service in company with LNWR and LNER catering cars. The BR1 and BR2 bogies that were fitted to the carriages in the previous two views were not entirely satisfactory. Ride quality deteriorated alarmingly after some time in traffic, and this was particularly marked with the heavier stock such as catering cars. One solution was the costly and very heavy Commonwealth bogie, which was fitted to SC1100. After trials in 1956-58, the Commonwealth bogie was adopted as standard until the proposed B4 bogie had been fully developed.

Top: In the Mk I era, BR accepted that some passengers liked compartment stock, whilst others preferred open vehicles. Trains frequently included both types. The Corridor First, or FK, was one response to travellers' wishes. W13277 was one of 50 Diagram 116 FKs built to Lot 30578 at Metropolitan-Cammell in 1960. We are looking at the corridor side of this Diagram 116 FK at Worcester (Shrub Hill) on 2nd July 1976. As with many Mk Is, the bottom of the side sheeting has corroded, and has been patched. The main cause was condensation getting trapped between the inner and outer body shells, and collecting at the base of the panel. The panel itself was welded to the pillars, but this caused damage to the preservative coating that was applied to the sheeting, making the panel vulnerable to corrosion at the very spot where water collected. W13277 is mounted on B4 bogies. The metal slots near the doors are to accept the metal coach letter plates, A, B, C, etc that were adopted on the Western Region, but the coach actually carries a paper label inside the windows.

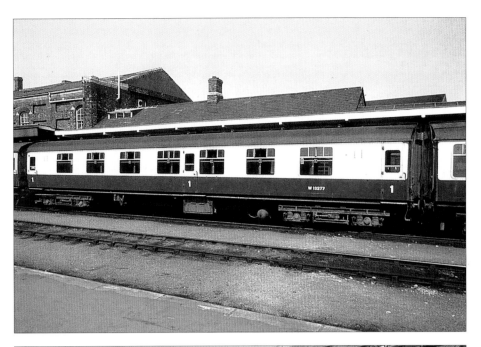

Centre: The Open First, FO, was built to Diagram 73. M3045 was one of 18 FOs built under Lot 30091 at Doncaster in 1954. Although built in the days of the BR1 bogie, M3045 sported B4 bogies by the time this view was taken at Rugby in July 1972. The B4 bogie had passed its trials in 1963, but as Mk I construction ended shortly thereafter in favour of the Mk II, few new coaches went into service with the B4. However many older Mk1s were refurbished with B4 bogies to improve riding qualities, especially if they were heavy vehicles such as catering cars, or were used on high speed routes such as the East or West Coast main lines. As several windows have been left open, it is likely that M3045 was a 'failure' and had been withdrawn from a set and dropped into the siding in a hurry. The near section is smoking, but the three further bays are non smoking, two with the old triangular 'No Smoking' label, one with the later circular label.

Bottom: The Open Third came in two varieties, the 48 seat TO, and the more cramped 64 seat Tourist Third Open, or TTO, the two types being re-designated SO and TSO when Third class was renamed. The idea behind the TSO was to provide a high capacity open vehicle, similar to the Gresley Tourist stock of the 1930s. M3767 was built to Diagram 93 under Lot 30079 at York in 1953. In 1985, the BR charter train unit refurbished a rake of Mk1s into chocolate and cream and a further rake into the green and cream livery used on the LNER Tourist stock. This set was intended for steam specials on the West Highland line. The use of Mk Is was short lived, as most had been replaced by Mk2s by the end of 1990. IC3767C, as M3767 had become, was purchased by the Glenfinnan Station Museum in 1991, where it is seen in West Highland Line livery. In these first six views of the Mk I, we have illustrated vehicles from seven different makers, carrying five different liveries, and mounted on four different types of bogie.

Top: The Diagram 56 Restaurant Third Open (RTO, later RSO) was a rare vehicle. Intended to run with kitchen cars or to supplement the seating capacity of kitchen-restaurant cars. Just 14 cars were built to this design. They emerged from York under Lot 30014 in 1951, and were numbered 1000-1013. Most went to the Western Region. Unlike the ordinary Open Thirds that had fixed seats, the Diagram 56 restaurant cars had loose chairs, with a 36 seat smoking section and a 12 seat non-smoking portion. There were no intermediate doors and both toilets were at the same end, on each side of the passage leading to the corridor connection. DW150353 began life as RTO W1012, but was converted to a cinema coach and renumbered in 1963. It is seen in this guise at Rugby on 13th June 1974. Later acquiring an additional Z prefix to the number, this former

WR vehicle could be found anywhere on the system, as it toured the rail network to show instructional and promotional films. It was preserved in 1990, going to the Great Central at Loughborough. The cinema coach is running with an SR bogie van, which has a label clipped in the frame, but the cinema coach itself has no label clip, so the label has been stapled to the footboard at the left hand end of the coach.

Above: Mk I gangwayed stock found use in other lands as well, most notably Ireland, where CIE acquired a batch of Mk Is for conversion to Brake Steam Heating Vans. Much of the CIE diesel fleet came from General Motors in America, and lacked steam heating boilers. To meet this need cheaply, CIE bought redundant BSKs and BCKs from British Rail. They were rebuilt by BREL at Derby Litchurch Lane works,

prior to being shipped to Ireland. All the passenger accommodation was removed, and the vacant space received a Lister HR3 generator developing 32.5 hp, and a Spanner boiler to provide steam heating. It was a curious experience when a CIE train departed from a station with a coach making noises reminiscent of a diesel locomotive. Irish Rail 3180TLA, formerly 3180w, had started life as E34378, and was built to Diagram 181 under Lot 30032 at Wolverton in 1952. No 3180 is seen running on Irish broad gauge (5ft 3in) B5 bogies at Cahir, on the former Waterford, Limerick & Western line in September 1996. The B5 bogie was a heavyweight version of the successful B4 design, and was necessary as the generator vans weighed over 37 tons.

Right: Between 1951 and 1963, over 1100 Gangwayed Brakes or BGs were produced to Diagram 711. A considerable number remained in service at the dawn of the twenty first century, 50 years after they had been designed. Others had gone into departmental service and more into preservation. Earlier in this book I referred to an ex works stock train at Rugby in 1964. Some 12 years later, I photographed a range of freshly painted stock outside Derby works. M81343 began life in 1958, as a part of Lot 30400. Often Lots could be for ten or fewer vehicles, but Lot 30400 was one of the largest Mk I orders placed. This covered Nos 81313 to 81497, and came from Pressed Steel, a company which was to receive other very large orders for rolling stock. It is seen ex works on 6th July 1976. The body is in rail blue, with the upper panel in pearl grey (BS colour 9-095). The roof is in dark grey (BS 9-089). In theory, the underframe and bogies were to be painted in chocolate brown, (BS 3-039) in recognition that these areas pick up a lot of brown road dirt, so a brown base colour makes sense. The bogies, battery boxes and brake gear are chocolate brown, but the solebars and headstocks are in rail blue, as are the wooden steps. Unlike passenger doors, which open outwards, the guard's door on the BG was hinged to open inwards. M81343, later 84343 was preserved in 1987, going to the Great Central Railway.

Below: Some of the most colourful vehicles on British Railways have been the TPOs. Branded 'Royal Mail' in elegant serif lettering until the 1960s, they went into drab rail blue and grey for twenty years, before re-emerging in dazzling Post Office red. The initial experiments took place in 1986, with plain red, but the addition of two yellow bands in 1987 made the vehicles far more eye catching. 80306 NSV is a Diagram 721 Post Office Sorting Van. Just three vehicles were built to Lot 30487 in 1959, as a variant on the more common Diagram 720. This had appeared in 1959, and early batches were fitted with the traditional TPO nets and arms to pick up and delivery mailbags at speed. However, the Diagram 721 vehicles were for duties where this facility was not needed. After 1971 when the lineside exchange of mail pouches was phased out, the nets and traducer arms were removed from vehicles to which they had been fitted. Following the so-called *great* train robbery in 1963, security on postal services was tightened up, and the windows received robust grills, as can be seen in this portrait of No 80306 at Lincoln on 3rd July 1989. Later batches of sorting carriages received smaller windows as a further security precaution.

Top: The Mk I GUV was a development of the ideas developed by R E L Maunsell in the 1920s, for a 'do anything, go anywhere, carry anything' vehicle. The prototype BR General Utility Van, No 86500, to Diagram 810, appeared in 1956. It had flat sides, unlike the passenger stock, end doors to make it suitable for cars and other vehicles, and two pairs of side doors for general traffic. After inviting staff comments, the production batches were provided to Diagram 811, with three sets of side doors. Over 900 were built. M86226 was from another large Pressed Steel order, (86078-499) built under Lot 30417 in 1958-59. It is seen at Derby on 6th July 1976, and has received all over rail blue livery, and 'Express Parcels' branding. Once again, the solebars and headstocks are rail blue rather than chocolate brown. The yellow spot at the right hand end of the body bears the inscription, 'Brute Circuit Only'. This was a dedicated service moving loaded platform trolleys or brutes (the acronym 'brute' stands for, British Railways Universal Transport Equipment), between designated centres to provide a high speed parcel service with low handling costs. Interestingly this vehicle also made it into preservation, going to Tunbridge Wells in 1991. As with the BG, it is a perfect 'ex works' photo.

Above: A short four-wheeled General Utility Van, E94100, was built to Diagram 815 in 1955. It was 30ft 9in over the body with a 20 foot wheelbase, but when series construction began in 1958, a new Diagram was issued. The Diagram 816 CCT, or Covered Carriage Truck, as it had become, was 37ft over headstocks, with a 23ft 6in wheelbase, and had two pairs of doors each side, instead of a single pair as on the Diagram 815 van. End doors were also provided. M94149, was built under Lot 30549. This covered no fewer than 200 CCTs, produced at Earlestown between 1958 and 1960. In the 30 miles from Wolverton works to Rugby, where I photographed it on 30th July 1964, not even the shock absorbers or axleguards had lost their gloss finish. It looks almost too clean to be real, but within a very few days, and particularly in bad weather, the underframe would have started to show greys and browns, and weathering would have begun. In the mid-1980s British Rail lost a great deal of parcels, mail and newspaper traffic, and the CCT fleet was eliminated by the end of 1988.

Top: The Mk I concept even embraced the carriage of horses, as horseboxes to Mk I standards were produced. No fewer than 115 vehicles to Diagram 751 were produced to Lot 30146 by Earlestown wagon works in 1958. Their principal employment was the conveyance of racehorses, and given the concentration of racecourses and leading stables around Newmarket on the Eastern Region, and on the Southern Region, the allocation reflected this. Nos 96300-304 went to the LMR, 96305-354 went to the ER, 96355-358 went to the WR, and 96359 to 96414 to the SR. The Southern painted its allocation green, the other regions using the standard maroon. The rapid transfer of racehorse traffic from rail to road meant that the business was dying out even as they were being built, and the last of the class was withdrawn in 1971. E96321 is seen at York in April 1967, together with an LNER Diagram 9 horsebox M2454E. This vehicle was built as late as 1954 at the ex-LNWR wagon works at Earlestown. Its numbering sequence indicates that it was allocated to the LM region,

hence the M prefix, but it was of LNER design, indicated by the E suffix. Because of this dual personality, it was also allocated D2181 in the former LMS Diagram book. It has to be admitted that the BR design is more elegant than the planked LNER vehicle, but one wonders why it was thought necessary to build such stock when the market was already in rapid decline.

Above: With a great deal of non-gangwayed stock inherited from the 'Big Four', and excellent designs available, there was no urgent need for Mk I non-corridor stock. Delivery of pre-nationalisation types continued into 1953, and the first Mk I suburban stock did not appear until 1954. The advent of the first DMUs that same year, plus the spread of electrification, meant that the production of Mk I non-corridor stock was small compared to gangwayed vehicles. When production did begin, a surprising range of designs evolved. They included compartment, open and lavatory stock, with passenger access to the lavatories via

corridors, but without gangways to connect to adjacent vehicles. E48007 was an SLO, or Lavatory Open Second, built to Diagram 330. It was on a short 57ft chassis and was built at Doncaster under Lot 30092 in 1955, one of 28 coaches built for Eastern Region suburban services. E48007 is seen at York in January 1969, shortly after it had been taken out of service. At least 11 of this small class were preserved. Most surprisingly, five consecutively numbered vehicles, 48006 to 48010 were all saved, but the fate of E48007 epitomised what happened to this group. Following a spell on the Worth Valley railway, E48007 went to Radstock about 1973, and was broken up three years later. By 1991 every one of these five consecutively numbered preserved carriages had been scrapped!

Top: Often thought of as wagons, milk tanks were built to coaching stock standards, as milk was a highly perishable commodity that required fast transit. Originally carried in churns in vehicles such as the GWR Siphon, there was a move in the 1920s and 1930s towards milk tanks. The first tanks were four-wheeled, but the better riding qualities of the six- wheel tank triumphed. W44551 was part of a sizeable batch (Nos 44512-561) built under Lot 1640 at Derby in 1950. It is to a BR LMR design, and is seen at Carlisle on 21st May 1977. According to the Diagram book, all fifty tanks of Lot 1640 were to Diagram D 2173, which had the filling hatch moved to one end, as the tank was sloped to allow certain impurities to settle. However this view of Western Region allocated tank W44551 shows a centrally positioned filler, a level tank, and a totally different ladder arrangement as well. Nos 44520 and 44546 were definitely to Diagram D 2173, but illustrations of W44555 and W44556 show them to have been similar to W44551, suggesting that the later tanks in this lot were not to Diagram D 2173, whatever the Diagram book might postulate. The tank is branded for Unigate Creameries Ltd. The end discharge point is clearly visible. Milk tanks put in a high daily mileage, many coming from the Scottish borders or Cumbria to London. By the time they had been loaded, sent many hundreds of miles, discharged and then internally cleaned, there was little time left for external cleaning, the modeller's vision of spotless milk tanks is far removed from reality.

Centre: By 1949, the GNR(I) was the last remaining independent trunk line in the British Isles. Despite rising costs, the company remained optimistic and had just taken delivery of superb new steam engines for the prestige Belfast-Dublin 'Enterprise' expresses. In 1947, the first two of the magnificent C2 class Corridor Firsts emerged from Dundalk works. In 1949 two more were completed, Nos 227 and 228. They were plated as being 60ft long by 9ft 6in wide and weighed 32.5 tons. Regarded by many who travelled on them as the finest coaches to have entered service in Ireland, they were almost the last of the breed. No 228, now N182 in the UTA fleet, is seen in the carriage sidings at Belfast's Great Victoria Street station on 26th August 1966.

Bottom: The Ulster Transport Authority began life on April Fool's Day 1948, an unfortunate date as things turned out, as the bus side of the new authority soon triumphed over the railways, which were savagely pruned. The LMS NCC had a mixed fleet of parcels stock, some going back to the 1890s. In 1946 the replacement V15 fitted van was introduced. They were 24ft long with unusual horizontally planked sides. UTA No1894 was one of 25 such vans completed up to 1949. This introduces a new carriage builder to these pages, Harland & Wolff of Belfast, better known as ship builders, their products including the ill-fated *Titanic*. Under the 1959 renumbering system, 1894 became 680, and is seen in UTA 'NCC Region' red livery at York Road station in September 1966.

SELF-PROPELLED STOCK

From the dawn of the railway age, it was clear that a lightweight engine and small coach would be ideal for inspection trains or lightly used services. The first person to develop such ideas was William Bridges Adams, who built a small steam railcar that was tested on the Eastern Counties Railway in 1847, and further cars for the Bristol & Exeter and ECR by 1849. They were in advance of existing technology and there was little further progress until 1902. Then, in less than a decade, with most of the activity concentrated in the first five years, just over 200 steam railcars appeared in the British Isles, spread across 25 different railways. The GWR, with a fleet of 99 cars, was the most thorough exponent, and the most successful. Its cars were well designed, most of them lasting into the 1930s. Some 78 of the GWR cars were converted into auto trailers for push pull working, and they established the body style for the Great Western auto coach that continued in production into BR days. Concurrently with the steam railcar craze, a much smaller petrol railcar mania swept the British Isles, though total production was just one twentieth of the steam fleet. However, in the decade prior to the Great War, the foundations had been laid, and a few good and many very bad railcars had been produced. In the 1920s, more steam railcars appeared of a totally different type. The most important design was the Sentinel, which used a geared high-speed steam engine. Numerous companies experimented with the Sentinel, but there was one predominant user, the LNER, the last of whose cars reached BR ownership. In the 1930s, the GWR, GNR(I) and LMS NCC all introduced diesel railcars, and had it not been for the outbreak of war in 1939, there would have been more progress. Development ended with the outbreak of hostilities and did not resume until well after the war. A few experimental railcars appeared in mainland Britain, but it was the GNR(I), that introduced the first diesel multiple unit trains in 1950. The UTA followed suit, as did BR, from 1954 onwards.

Top: At the behest of its general manager, Oliver Bury, the Great Northern Railway was one of the first to experiment with a petrol engined railcar, trying a Daimler-engined car built by Dick, Kerr & Co. It was not satisfactory, so the GNR loco engineer, H A Ivatt, opted for steam railcars. Six were built, two at Doncaster, two by Kitson and two by Avonside. They entered service in 1905-06, and because of their diminutive steam engines, were more economical to run that a conventional steam set. These savings came at a price, for the railcar was too weak a pull a laden trailer, and on some steeply graded routes, was barely capable

of moving itself. This was the problem that faced all designers, for the economy came from the use of a small steam engine, and if the engine was large enough to have spare capacity, the bulk of the potential savings vanished. By 1918, all six cars were stored out of use. Refurbished in 1922-23, they saw limited use, but were withdrawn in 1925-26 and the engine portions broken up. This contemporary coloured view by E Pouteau is of GN steam car No 2. The coach portion was the first vehicle to have been designed by the recently appointed carriage and wagon superintendent, H N Gresley and shows all the hallmarks of the Gresley design. After the engines were scrapped, all six carriage sections saw further use.

Above: The first petrol-engined railcars were built by the North Eastern Railway in 1903, although teething troubles delayed their introduction into service until 1904. Further cars appeared on the LBSCR, the GNR and elsewhere. By 1914, eleven passenger railcars had appeared on the standard and broad gauge railways of Britain and Ireland. With the exception of the NER cars, none were long-lived or successful. In Ireland, there was one remarkable narrow-gauge car. It was built in 1906 by the Birmingham based firm of Allday & Onions for the County Donegal Railways Joint

Committee. This was the year the system acquired new owners, as it was bought jointly by the powerful Midland Railway and its other neighbour, the GNR(I). When Henry Forbes took over as manager in 1910, he was not impressed with the railcar. A 22hp engine replaced its original engine in 1920 and an enclosed body was fitted, which seated 6-10 persons. Thus altered, it was used on inspection duties. It came into its own during the prolonged miners' strike of 1926 which disrupted coal supplies. Forbes used the railcar on the long but lightly used Glenties branch, saving a steam engine. He soon realised he had a vehicle that could cut running costs dramatically. Within weeks he was looking for larger cars to convert. By 1933, the CDR had a mixed fleet of petrol and diesel cars which were operating a large part of its timetabled services. In 1925, the motive power costs on the Donegal had been £15,378 for 225,220 train miles, all steam worked. By 1935, train mileage had risen to 419,395, an 86% increase, but with railcars working over 75% of services, costs had fallen to £10,295. Seldom in transport history had there been such a dramatic turn-round. No 1 received a replacement petrol engine in 1949, and after withdrawal was preserved at the Belfast Transport Museum, where it is seen on 1st September 1964.

Left: The Sentinel *Waggon* Works Ltd of Shrewsbury was a successful manufacturer of steam road vehicles, using a small vertical boiler with prodigious steam raising abilities. This was the Super-Sentinel engine. Transmission was via a chain drive. Sensing a new market on the railways, Sentinel developed a small four-wheel steam shunting engine at the start of the 1920s, and in conjunction with Cammell Laird & Co of Nottingham, developed a lightweight steam railcar. The first Sentinel railcar was built for the 3ft 6in gauge Jersey Railways & Tramways, and its success prompted the neighbouring Jersey Eastern Railway to order a pair of standard gauge Sentinel cars as well. At the February 1926 annual general meeting of the JER, the manager, Major Gilbert More, announced that a Sentinel car was on order. When it arrived, I expect that the manager's young son Kenneth, had an enjoyable time looking at the latest addition to his father's full sized train set. Kenneth would grow up to become one of Britain's best known and celebrated actors, appearing in such memorable 1950s films as *Reach for the Sky* and *Sink the Bismarck*. Two cars were delivered to the JER, named *Normandy* and *Brittany*, but despite the savings they permitted, both island railways were to succumb, the JER in 1929 and the JR&T a few years later. The body of *Brittany* became a summerhouse in Jersey, but the locomotive unit was shipped to England in 1929 and put to work in Chatham dockyard as a shunting engine. It moved to Peters of Merstham in 1935, and then to the Standard Brick & Sand Co near Redhill. In 1962, by which time it was known as *Dom*, it was presented to the newly formed Kent & East Sussex Railway Preservation Society. She arrived at Tenterden on 15th June 1962. Never steamed on the K&ESR, but used as a brake van, *Dom* became one of the forgotten legion of preserved engines, which was sad, given its historic significance. This historic but unfortunate relic of the Sentinel era is seen on the K&ESR on 26th June 1968.

Above: In 1924, the Sentinel Waggon Works exhibited a railcar at the British Empire Exhibition at Wembley. My father visited the exhibition as a 12 year old, and Gresley's *Flying Scotsman* and the GWR *Caerphilly Castle* left a lifelong impression. He also spoke about other railway exhibits, including the half engine-half coach Sentinel railcar. Another visitor to the exhibition was Nigel Gresley, and he too was impressed, so much so, that the LNER acquired no fewer than 81 Sentinel railcars in less than ten years. They were to several different types, reflecting design improvements between successive orders, and the decision to name most of them after old-fashioned horse-drawn stagecoaches was a brilliant publicity move. In 1927, Sentinel began work on a trial car to an improved design, and this was delivered to the LNER the following spring as No 2133. Accepted into LNER stock, given a new number, 35, and named *Nettle*, this prototype six cylinder gear and shaft drive car was the only one of its type, built to LNER diagram 93, as the production batch differed somewhat. Prior to the delivery of *Nettle*, the Sentinel cars had appeared in a bewildering array of liveries, but the well known green and cream livery was introduced on this car, and spread to the rest of the fleet and to the 1930s articulated Tourist Open stock. Despite offering considerable economies, delivery of spares could be protracted, and the lightweight engine was more prone to failure than conventional steam engines. Where loads fluctuated greatly, the cars were unsuitable due to their limited ability to haul additional vehicles. Withdrawal began in 1939, and finished in 1948. *Nettle* lasted until August 1945.

Right: The Great Western Railway is customarily credited with introducing diesel railcars into regular passenger service in the British Isles. In reality, the premier place goes to the County Donegal Railways, with railcars Nos 7 and 8 which entered traffic in 1931. In July 1932, the GNR(I) introduced its first diesel railcar, 'A'. On the 3ft gauge Clogher Valley Railway in Northern Ireland, a new type of railcar entered service in 1932. When the CVR closed at the end of 1941, this was bought by the CDRJC, becoming their No 10. Also in 1932, the LMS NCC built railcar No 1, which entered traffic in January 1933. Three more LMS NCC cars followed, No 4 entering service in 1938. All four NCC cars were powered by two Leyland 125 hp diesel engines driving through hydraulic transmissions with Lysholm Smith torque converters. Nos 3 and 4 had a rated top speed of 72.6 mph. No 4 was 63 ft 6in long with raised driving positions at each end. Unlike many early railcars, the NCC cars were sufficiently powerful to convey tail traffic or a trailer coach, and the NCC converted an elderly six wheel carriage to serve as a railcar trailer. Rather than go to the expense of cabling to a remote driving position, NCC cars 2, 3 and 4 were fitted with raised turrets, so that the driver could look out over the roof of the 6-wheeler as the railcar propelled it along at 70 mph! The view could not have been very good, but NCC staff loved to tell how all went well until the day that the trailer encountered a cow. The resultant derailment must count as a moral victory for the cow, and the practice of propelling six wheelers at high speed ended. We see the astonishing railcar No 4 at York Road, Belfast on 27th August 1967. Sadly this historic vehicle later suffered fire damage, and was cut up in December 1969.

Bottom: The GNR(I) had no ambitions to propel six-wheel carriages at high speeds backwards, but they were keen to develop a railcar set, rather than a single unit. In 1936, cars D and E were produced. They comprised a

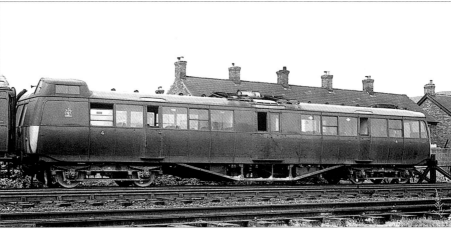

short central engine section mounted on top of a six-coupled power bogie, to which passenger saloons were articulated at each end. The railcar was powered by a 153 BHP Gardner 6L3 diesel engine, which was a mistake, for the engine was incapable of delivering sufficient power to the coupled wheels to offer a really lively performance. In fact, the top speed in fourth gear was just 42 mph. In 1938, for railcars F and G, the GNR modified the format. Once again there was a central power unit, but instead of a six-coupled power bogie, there were two independent axles, each driven by a 102 bhp Gardner 6LW diesel, via a Vulcan-Sinclair hydraulic coupling. In 1958 one went north and the other went south, but was later sold to the UTA. Railcar F became UTA No 104, and is seen at Warrenpoint on 1st September 1964. The unusual buffers and articulated power bogie are clearly visible. When we were talking to the driver, he explained one of the peculiarities of F and G. The unit could be controlled from either cab, but the engine forward/reverse selectors were in the powerhouse. After arriving at a terminus, the driver left what had been the leading cab, walked through the unit, and turned the selector on the first engine he encountered to reverse. At the far end of the

powerhouse, there was a second engine and direction selector, but this would already be in **reverse**. He turned this to forward. Then he could go to what would now be the leading end, and start the car. Both wheels would now rotate in the same direction, If the driver set both selectors to forward, the wheels would start out in opposite directions, as each wheel was of the opinion that forward meant moving the passenger saloon at its end of the unit forward. If both selectors were reverse, then instead of trying to tear the car apart, the wheels attempted to squash it together. In response to my father's enquiry if this did not confuse new drivers, the driver responded in a rich Ulster accent that this was not unknown, and whenever a new man was entrusted with No 104, the seasoned staff gathered round to enjoy the proceedings. I was never quite convinced of this, but years later, I found documentary evidence that No 104 was so blessed! As the driving cab was a tiny cubicle occupying just the centre window out of the three nose windows, it was possible to get excellent ahead views as well. That, plus the ability to start in opposite directions simultaneously, made 104 my all time favourite railcar. It was withdrawn in November 1965.

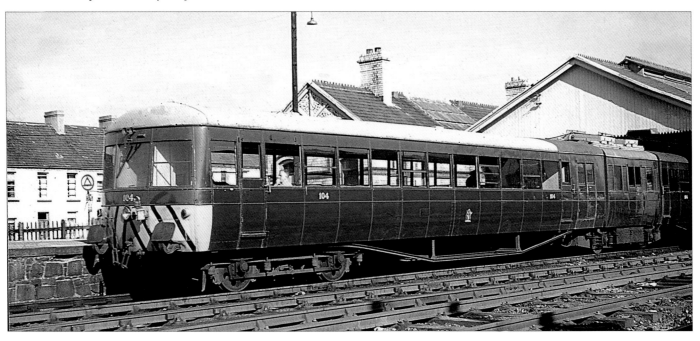

Above: The GNR(I) had some lines where the potential traffic was so light, that even a one coach railcar was excessive. They also operated road buses, and the engineers at Dundalk were resourceful men. They took a couple of redundant single deck buses, mounted them on railway wheels, and created some stylish railbuses. Colonel Holman F Stephens had done so in the early 1920s on some of his light railways, but the results were not very successful or long-lived. The LMS experimented with the Karrier Ro-Railer which was a convertible rail/road bus, which could transform itself on a special length of track. This did not last long either. By contrast, the GNR(I) built three railbuses for itself, two for the Dundalk, Newry & Greenore Railway, both of which later went to the GNR, and two for the Sligo, Leitrim & Northern Counties Railway. The GN trio entered service in 1934-35. They were 'numbered' D, E and F, but when the articulated railcars came along, they became D1, E2 and F3. Railbus E2 later became No 1 and in 1956 was transferred to departmental stock as 8178. It is seen at Grosvenor Road goods depot, Belfast on 30th August 1964. Thankfully it was preserved and went to the Belfast Transport Museum, and later to Cultra. The rear wheel may puzzle the observant reader. It looks like a rubber road tyre with a steel rail tyre on the outside. This is exactly what it is! The Howden-Meredith patent wheel was specially developed for the GNR railbuses to improve their riding. Unlike the Colonel Stephens' railbuses which were operated back-to-back, the GN railbuses were operated singly. Passengers entered or left the bus via a platform at the rear, with steps for ground level halts.

Above: The end of the Second World War found the railways of Britain badly run down as a result of wartime arrears of maintenance and enemy action. With iron, steel, coal, oil, and timber all in short supply, refurbishment was bound to be slow, and attention was directed to the most pressing tasks. In 1945-46, diesel railcars had a low priority, and by 1947, the 'Big Four' faced the looming threat of nationalisation. When the Railway Executive came to power, their focus was on fundamental problems, so it was not until 1951 that a Lightweight Trains committee was set up to examine the use of railcars. As in the 1930s, it was not the big British lines, but the cash-strapped Irish railways that moved first. In 1950-51, the CDRJC acquired two diesel mechanical railcars. The power bogie, which had coupling rods, was produced by Walker Bros of Wigan, and was powered by a Gardner 6LW diesel driving via a mechanical gearbox. The bodywork was produced by the GNR(I) works at Dundalk, and the passenger section was articulated to the cab unit, providing a highly flexible vehicle. This system had been developed in the 1930s, and applied to the pre-war bogie cars for the County Donegal, and also to vehicles built for export. No 19 arrived in January 1950, and No 20 in January 1951. They each cost about £8,000, and seated 41 passengers. No 20 is seen at Killybegs station ready to depart with a midday service to Donegal Town. The CDRJC closed on 31st December 1959. Railcars 19 and 20 were purchased by the Isle of Man Railway, and were well maintained until the late 1980s but were then neglected. A rebuild commenced at the end of the 1990s, but is presently on hold. It would be wonderful to see these cars run again.

Above: The LMS had a habit of 'trying it on the dog' as far as the NCC was concerned, and after assessing the NCC results with hydraulic transmission and torque converters, the LMS built a stylish semi-streamlined three-car articulated railcar in 1938. After testing, it entered passenger service early in 1939. It was powered by six 125 hp diesel engines, each driving a single axle via a torque converter. Sadly, many of the lessons from the NCC were not heeded. The engines were mounted vertically on the centre line of the coach, and because of the side skirting and other components, were difficult to reach for servicing. The radiators were mounted between the frames, so were screened from direct draught. Scoops were provided, but were of doubtful value, and this system was never repeated. The set was 182 feet long, and was finished in a striking red and ivory livery with a silver grey roof. It was numbered 80000-80002 in the coaching stock series, and is seen departing from Euston. When it went into regular service, it was allocated to Bedford, and operated through services on the secondary line between Oxford and Cambridge, completing the 77-mile journey in 105 minutes. The set gained a reputation for unreliability, and was later used between St Pancras and Bedford, sometimes working through to Nottingham. By 1940, the LMS had more pressing problems to cope with, and it was placed in store. In 1949, it was converted to a two-car diesel maintenance set for the Altrincham electric line.

Right: The Great Western had started its diesel railcar programme a few months after the GNR(I) and the LMS NCC. By 1942 it was operating the largest railcar fleet in the British Isles with 38 vehicles in service. Unlike the LMS triplet, above, the design was superb. All cars used AEC equipment, with the chassis and bodies by Park Royal, Gloucester Railway Carriage & Wagon Co, or Swindon. The GW fleet constituted more than half of the diesel railcars operating in the British Isles. In 1954 or 1955, I saw one of the new Derby lightweight units. A few days later, we visited Leamington Spa, and one of the GWR diesel railcars came in. I am fairly sure that it was W22W, the subject of this photo. This, to my youthful mind, was style, and I immediately concluded that the green Derby lightweights had been found wanting, and the next generation of diesel railcars would be stylish vehicles like W22W, which was resplendent in carmine and cream. This was not quite right, of course, as W22W had entered service as far back as 18th September 1940, but it does show the clarity of vision of youth, as the GW cars had real elegance. W22W was preserved by the Great Western Society but was loaned to the Severn Valley Railway from 1967 to 1978. It is seen at Bridgnorth station on 22nd May 1971, after restoration to GWR chocolate and cream with a shirt button logo.

Above: After a resume of progress in Ireland, I would have liked to cover developments on BR, but in 1950, BR had not even formed its lightweight trains committee, so all the progress was between AEC, Park Royal and the Irish drawing offices. The UTA had inherited the four LMS NCC cars, and as the GN cars were being built, the UTA ordered equipment from AEC for what must have been the most unusual DMU ever built. If you were to ask most enthusiasts if a fully panelled DMU had ever operated in public service, the likely answer would be no. To trim costs for its new train, the UTA decided to rebuild a pair of pre-war coaches. Nine class J10 Open Thirds, Nos 201-209 had been built in 1936-39, with a panelled body, derived from the LMS Period 2 style. Nos 205 and 207 were rebuilt as power cars with driving cabs at one end. Instead of using vertical diesel engines, the J10s would each receive a pair of AEC horizontal 125 bhp diesels, driving through fluid couplings and four-speed gearboxes. A panelled class J7 coach was converted to act as an intermediate car in the set, and the train entered service in August 1951. It proved successful, and when the UTA took over the former GNR lines in Northern Ireland in 1958, it was often found on that part of the UTA system. Car No 6, former NCC Open Third No 205, is seen at York Road station, Belfast on 27th August 1967. Following fire damage, it was broken up in December 1969. Again, what a tragic loss.

Top: AEC had collaborated with the GWR in producing the pre-war streamlined Great Western railcars, and in the 1940s developed a basic multiple unit system, which enabled a driver to control two power cars. In 1948, the GNR(I) placed an order with AEC for 20 power cars with the bodies to be built by Park Royal Vehicles and Dundalk works. Each power car was fitted with two 125hp AEC A215 vertical diesel engines, driving via a mechanical transmission, using a five-speed pre-selective gearbox. The power cars were delivered between June 1950 and April 1951. The intermediate cars for each three car set were converted from existing steel bodied passenger carriages. The GNR(I) was leading the way for the second time in twenty years, with the first significant diesel multiple unit fleet in the British Isles. Aesthetically, the GNR's Nos 600-619 were amongst the most elegant DMUs ever built, although they were always called railcars, and not DMUs on the GN. When the former GNR stock was divided in 1958, No 611 went north, becoming UTA No 115. It is seen on a six car Dublin express working between Belfast Central Junction and Adelaide on 25th August 1966. Sadly the whole class vanished in the 1970s, No 115 being scrapped at Antrim in May 1975.

Right: In the 1930s, commercial road vehicle builders such as Leyland and AEC had entered the railcar field. After the war, there were several complex reorganisations, which need to be explained. In 1946, Leyland and AEC formed a subsidiary company to work together on production of trolleybuses, and later of railcars. It was known as British United Traction, or BUT. Although popularly known as AEC, the Southall based company was actually entitled, 'The Associated Equipment Co'. In 1948, AEC became a holding company and was renamed Associated Commercial Vehicles, or ACV. Vehicle manufacturing was transferred to a subsidiary company within the ACV group, which took the short title of AEC. In 1949 Park Royal Vehicles, which had a long association with AEC, became part of the ACV group. By this time, AEC and Leyland were very unhappy with the stagnation over railcar development on BR. They felt that the lack of home orders harmed their reputation and export chances. Using the BUT name, they decided to force the issue, and as a private venture, built eleven four wheeled lightweight railbuses. There were eight power cars, four being Driving Motor Seconds, and four having a brake compartment as well. There were also three Trailer Seconds, so they could run as one, two or three-car sets. A three-car set weighed 40.5 tons and could seat 110 passengers. The cars were 37ft 6in long and the power cars were fitted with an AEC 125bhp diesel engine.Commonly referred to as the BUT cars, they were also known as ACV cars on account of their AEC components. During the early trials they appeared on suburban services in the Birmingham area, operating out of Birmingham Moor St, and on the Gerrards Cross line. They also were used on the Harrow to Belmont branch and finally on the Watford-St Albans line where they spent most of their career. We see one of the experimental sets about to depart from Moor Street station in 1952. After a period of evaluation, they were taken into BR stock, but by 1961 were mostly out of use, being officially withdrawn in 1963.

Bottom: The next step forward was on the Ulster Transport Authority. They decided to introduce 14 three-car Multi-Engined Diesel or MED sets, involving 42 vehicles in all. Eight power cars would be completely new, as would the 14 trailers, but the remaining power cars were rebuilds from existing steam stock. As with cars Nos 6/7, each power car was fitted with a pair of horizontal 125bhp engines, with power being transmitted through a Lysholm-Smith hydraulic torque converter. Apart from controlling the engines within a set, the sets were designed to operate in multiple, so the driver could be controlling up to eight engines in four power cars. This posed serious problems in designing the control circuits. Previously, power cars had to be north-facing or south-facing. If a north-facing car failed, a south-facing car could not be turned to replace it, and vice versa, as the control system would not then work. Major Frank Pope, who had been manager of the LMS NCC in 1941-43, and first chairman of the UTA, from 1948 to 1951, had

taken a keen interest in solving this problem, and a spiral wiring harness was designed. Under this system, the No 2 engine start button would start the No 2 engine irrespective of the way that the cars were marshalled. Likewise the No 6 stop button would always stop the No 6 engine. This set, at Bangor on the County Down section of the UTA in September 1966, consists of cars 29, 509 and 28. The power cars 28 and 29 were both new in December 1952, 28 being a Driving Motor Brake Composite and 29 a Driving Third. Trailer car 509 was new in July 1953. All were buried at Crosshill Quarry in County Antrim in 1980! This was not some strange pagan ritual performed by railcar worshippers, but because the bodies were asbestos lagged, and new rules in the 1970s demanded special disposal facilities, interment in a flooded quarry was the most economic method of disposal. The middle car carries the short-lived 'County Down' region green and cream livery.

Above: The BR Lightweight Trains committee reported back in 1952, endorsing the development of DMUs, a proposal that was strongly backed by R C Bond, the member of the Railway Executive responsible for mechanical engineering. Major Frank Pope had become a member of the British Transport Commission in 1951, so UTA expertise in control circuits was available to British Railways in time to influence the first generation BR DMUs. In November 1952, Derby works received orders to build some two and three cars sets for Yorkshire and Cumberland. The two-car Yorkshire sets featured the Lysholm-Smith torque converter, but the decision by Leyland to discontinue production of this transmission on the road vehicle side made it uneconomic to produce, so later cars used a straight mechanical transmission instead. Leyland or AEC engines were used for different batches of car, whilst seating capacity and other facilities also varied. The body style was based on the BR Mk I passenger carriage, though there were slight differences, the side windows

being slightly lower than the Mk I. The ends were bow fronted, with large cab front windows, which earned the cars the nickname of Cathedrals or Glasshouses. M79666 and M79132 are seen at Aspley Guise on the Bletchley-Bedford line on 7th April 1967. M79666 is a Driving Trailer Composite Lavatory car, built to Lot 30202 for the LM Region in 1955. The far car, M79132, was built to Lot 30240, which was completed in 1954-55. It is a Driving Motor Brake Second, and was fitted with two 150bhp BUT (Leyland) engines. The cars were 57ft 6in long, the power cars weighing 27 tons, whilst the trailers weighed just 21 tons, these figures justifying the 'lightweight' description. The move from a semi-hydraulic transmission to an all mechanical system meant that the earliest cars were not compatible with later cars, and further design changes produced still more confusion. To obviate the risk of incompatible vehicles being coupled together, a colour coding system was developed, these vehicles becoming, 'Yellow Diamond' cars.

Opposite page, bottom: The Oxford-Bletchley-Cambridge branch once provided a convenient cross country route connecting the GWR, GCR, LNWR, Midland, GNR and GE lines radiating out of London. At Verney Junction, a branch line ran northwest to Buckingham and on to Banbury. Traffic was light, especially on the northern section, and with just three services a day each way, it was reputed to be losing about £14,000 per annum by 1956. In a rare mood of determination, BR built two railcars which were

intended to operate as single units. It was a unique instance of DMU stock being specially designed for one minor line. The two cars, M79900 and M79901, were built to two different lots, (30380 and 30387 respectively) and were basically a Lightweight Driving Motor Brake Second with an additional driving cab at what would be the inner end on an ordinary Driving Motor coach. There were slight external differences in the cars. The railcar service began on 13th August 1956. A more frequent service was provided, and operating costs fell by 30% over the next three years whilst traffic quadrupled. The operating pattern was slightly odd, as the two cars alternated daily on the Banbury-Buckingham section, where they made end on connection with a steam rail motor. Alas, even these results could not stave off closure, and services ended in January 1961. M79900 later became the legendary 'Test Coach Iris', RDB975010, of the Railway Technical Centre, Derby, and is seen in the special departmental livery at Aylesbury in 1989.

Below: The long pause in diesel train construction, from 1939 to 1954, meant that the Derby Lightweight cars had only just entered service when the 1955 Modernisation Plan burst upon the railways. Instead of a period of evaluation, which would allow detailed design improvements for later cars, the pace of change accelerated. The modernisation plan envisaged replacing the vast fleet of passenger tank locos and suburban stock with DMUs. Whilst the Derby Lightweights were still emerging from the works, the drawing offices were finalising plans

for what were to become the High Density or suburban sets. The Western Region wanted stock on 63ft 5in chassis, as with the Mk I gangwayed stock, and construction of the Derby High Density sets began in 1957. By the time M50071, M59008 and M50106 were photographed shunting forward out of the up platform at Leamington Spa station on 3rd July 1964, the ex Great Western lines in the Birmingham area had been transferred to the LM Region, but the set with its green livery and speed whiskers is pure WR. The nearest car, M50071, was one of 42 Driving Motor Brake Seconds (50050-91), and has the early four-lamp front. (Later cars had differing types of reporting number apertures). Unlike the Lightweights, this car weighed no less than 35.5 tons. The centre car, M59008, is a Trailer Composite, seating 28 First and 74 Second class passengers. The third vehicle, M50106 is a 95 seat Driving Motor Second. The Western Region three-car high density sets survived into the TOPS era, becoming class 116. They carry the 'blue square' or standard coupling code indication, which covered the majority of DMU classes.

record in the 1930s and 1940s, it is surprising they fared so badly in the 1950s bonanza. Just 20 two-car Low Density sets were produced in 1957. The Low Density terminology meant that the sets were to offer more comfort than on the High Density sets which were for heavily loaded commuter routes. The 'Park Royal' sets were built not at the PRV works in London, but at the Stockport works which had formerly belonged to Crossley Motors, a well-known bus and trolley bus builder, but which was by then a part of PRV. Although the Western Region wanted cars built to the Mk I corridor stock length of 63ft 5in, the LMR preferred 57ft units. As the PRV cars were for the LM, they conformed to this requirement. Twenty Driving Motor Brake Seconds were produced, and worked with a matching set of Driving Trailer Composite Lavatory cars. The motor cars were fitted with a pair of AEC 150 bhp engines, and most of the class were allocated to Chester. Known as class 103 under the TOPs scheme, Driving Motor car M50409 enters Newtown station on the Cambrian main line en route to Shrewsbury on 27th August 1973. The Chester depot number, CR218, is displayed in the left hand window. By this time only about half the class were still active, as the bodies had developed structural weaknesses. They were withdrawn by the mid-eighties.

Above: As the 1955 Modernisation plan was being finalised, the BRB was considering its implications. These included the rapid construction of up to 4,600 diesel railcars. This was far in excess of the capacity of BR's own works, so private builders were invited to submit designs and tenders. A golden age dawned for the rolling stock manufacturers, and Cravens, Metropolitan Cammell, Park Royal, Pressed Steel, Birmingham Railway Carriage & Wagon, Gloucester, and D Wickham all snapped up contracts. With the exception of Park Royal and Wickham, cars were ordered by the hundreds. Given Park Royal's distinguished

Opposite page, below: The Gloucester Railway Carriage & Wagon Co was another firm that had been involved in the GWR railcar programme in the 1930s. Gloucester built 200 cars to the 57ft 6in and 64ft 6in body lengths. Perhaps the most interesting were the twenty single-unit power cars produced by Gloucester in 1958 under Lot 30419. Numbered 55000-55019, they started their career on the Western region with a W prefix, but when the Birmingham lines of the GWR were transferred to LM control, gained an M prefix. Initially fitted with AEC engines, some cars later received Leyland engines. M55012 is seen at Stratford on Avon on 13th September 1971. They seated 65 Second class passengers and were used on routes such as the shuttle from Stourbridge Junction to Stourbridge Town and from Leamington to Stratford. This car carries Tyseley depot's rather untidy depot number in the front window. Unlike the PRV cars, they were long-lived and highly successful, and ABB Doncaster converted M55012 to give further service as a Route Learning car in 1995.

Above right: The Southern Region with its long history of suburban three-rail electrification preferred to electrify much of its network, or where this was not possible, to build diesel electric multiple units or DEMUs, rather than to adopt the mechanical or hydro-mechanical transmissions used elsewhere on BR. There were three main types of stock, the 'Hastings' units, which were slightly narrower than normal stock due to restricted tunnel clearances on that route, the normal width Berks and Hants units and the East Sussex cars which were to an intermediate width. In 1957, 18 two-car Hampshire sets were introduced. The Southern Region allocated set numbers, and the 2H sets became 1101-1118. Four more two-car sets, Nos 1119-1122 came in 1958. Unlike the DMUs, where the engines were underfloor, the powered DEMU cars included a vast engine compartment, and depending on the size of the luggage section, seated between 42 and 52 passengers. This was a low capacity, given the 63ft 5in frames on which they were mounted. In 1959, the original sets, 1101-1118 were strengthened to three coaches with the addition of a Trailer Open Second in each set. Sets 1119-1122 remained in their 2H format. Today, Alresford is an important station on the preserved Watercress line, but when this view was taken on 27th July 1972, it was a BR branch line under sentence of death. The driver of set 1121 waits for set 1122 to clear the single track section, so he can proceed on his way. The leading vehicle on set 1122 is a Driving Trailer Composite Lavatory (DTCL). The two car sets became TOPS class 204, and the three car sets became class 205. In later years there was a good deal of reorganisation, but forty years after their introduction, DEMUs were still a feature of the small number of non electrified lines in the south east of England.

Above: By the late 1950s, it was clear that there were many branch lines where traffic was so light that even the single unit cars used on the Buckingham branch were too large and costly for the available traffic. In a last flowering of the traditional public service mentality before the onslaught of the Beeching axe, BR bought 22 small four-wheel railbuses from five different makers. The most interesting batch were five vehicles produced by AC Cars, a firm better known for invalid cars and high performance racing cars. The railcars, W79975-9, were built in 1958 to Lot 30479. They were powered by a 150 bhp AEC engine with a mechanical transmission, and seated 46 passengers, and were the smallest and lightest of the 1958 railbuses. The absence of conventional buffers and couplings gives them an unusual appearance. Sadly even vehicles as economical as this could not grant a reprieve to many lines once the closure bug bit, and the cars rapidly found their scope for employment dwindling. Most migrated to Scotland, but had a very short life. W79978, which was built to Diagram 614, was preserved on the North Yorkshire Moors Railway in 1968 and is seen at Grosmont in June 1969. In 1979 it went to the K&ESR, and later to the Colne Valley Railway. It was a brave experiment, and if there had been more support from government, and less butchery of the rail network, it might have been a success.

Above: Although the Western Region had selected three-car High Density sets, the LM Region wanted four-car sets. Two types were introduced in the late 1950s, the class 115 diesel mechanical sets with Albion engines for the Marylebone services, and the class 127 St Pancras units. The St Pancras sets required high acceleration, and to achieve this, the Driving Motor Brake Seconds received two 238 bhp Rolls Royce diesel engines per power car. Given this exceptional power output, a hydraulic torque converter transmission was adopted, giving the cars excellent performance, but at the cost of making them incompatible with the common 'blue square' control system. The St Pancras sets, which were built at Derby in 1959, were given a red triangle coding. As high carrying capacity was important on this busy route, the St Pancras sets did not have First class accommodation. Driving Motor M51641 is the leading car as this class 127 unit enters Flitwick station on 7th October 1971. At this time, the line was still mechanically signalled with boxes dating from Midland times. Electrification of the Bedford-St Pancras section, and the appearance of the celebrated 'Bedpan' sets, rendered them surplus, and as the power cars were worn out, they were withdrawn. The trailers were refurbished and transferred to the Birmingham area to replace asbestos-lined trailers in class 116 DMUs.

Bottom: Two of the GWR railcars built in the 1930s and early 1940s were intended for 'Express Parcels' work in the London area, which permitted a reduction in station times for regular passenger services. When mass production of DMUs was approved as a result of the 1955 Modernisation Plan, the Western Region demanded more parcels cars for London and also for Birmingham. Six Driving Motor Luggage Vans were ordered for the WR, and a further four for the Manchester area of the LM Region. W55991-96 were built under Lot 30551 by the Gloucester Railway Carriage & Wagon Co for the WR, and delivered in 1959. They weighed 41 tons, a far cry indeed from the lightweight cars of just a few years earlier. The WR cars were fitted with gangways so that when they ran in multiple, parcels could be sorted en route. The LMR saw no need for this, and its cars were built without corridor connections. Four of the WR cars were sent to the West Midlands, and on the transfer of the ex GWR lines around Birmingham to the LMR, they passed to LM control. M55993 was one of the cars transferred to LM rule, hence its M prefix. The car is seen amongst the magnificent hybrid GWR-LNWR signals at Shrewsbury on 30th June 1976. The LMR did not like the corridor connections and later removed them, but this had not happened to M55993 at this time. Once again, the weathering on the power bogies and other visible underframe components is a mixture of rust, road dirt and mud. They became TOPS class 128.

Above: After the years of stagnation from 1947 to 1952, when the only progress with railcars had been in Ireland, the deluge of new cars and new designs that commenced on BR in 1954 eclipsed what the railways of Ireland were doing. However, the Great Northern Railway Board continued to make progress until its demise in 1958, whilst the Ulster Transport Authority introduced its Multi Purpose Diesel trains from 1957 onwards. Once again, the UTA followed its own idiosyncratic approach, creating power cars from older loco hauled stock. Driving Motor Brake Second No 49 was rebuilt from the unique class K7 Brake Second of 1951, No 351. It was powered by an 0900 Leyland 275 bhp engine, and with the demise of the Lysholm Smith torque converter, a Schneider hydraulic torque converter was used instead. MPD car No 49 is seen at York Road depot, Belfast on 27th August 1967. Built as compartment stock, it was converted to an open layout in 1970. It is in the V band version

of the maroon and ivory NCC section livery. It was later converted back to loco hauled stock operating on excursion sets behind the Northern Ireland Railways 101 class Bo-Bo locomotives.

Below: The Western Region decided that some routes required something better than the Low Density units, and proposed a DMU with First and Second class seating, luggage space and catering facilities. The result was the Swindon Cross County Unit. Three batches were built; 49 sets for the Western Region in 1958, seven for the Scottish Region in 1959 and a final 9 for the WR in 1961. Each power car received two AEC 150 bhp engines. M51585, from the final WR batch is seen passing Smethwick West Junction signal box on 2nd July 1976. It became class 120 under the TOPS scheme. In 1956, there had been just over 150 DMU power cars on BR. By 1958, there were over 1,400, and DMUs were operating almost 40% of total passenger train

mileage. The units had succeeded in attracting many additional passengers to rail, and their running costs were a third of those of steam trains. However the losses continued to grow, and Dr Beeching was brought in to re-organise BR. He axed both lightly used and uneconomic route and valuable lines as well. As the network contracted, DMUs were switched from lines that had been dieselised and then closed, to other sections, and the need for new stock came to an end. The last DMUs were built in 1963. Out of the planned 4,600 railcars, 4171 had been produced between 1954 and 1963. Almost a quarter of a century would elapse before a new generation of units began to supplant them. When they came into service in the 1950s and early 60s, the enthusiasts of the day hated them, yet in the twilight of their career in the 1990s, a new generation of enthusiasts called them 'Heritage' units and chased them with the same dedication that the steam engines they had supplanted had once been followed.

ELECTRIC PASSENGER STOCK

Steam and diesel locomotives or railcars work very differently, but they all generate their own power. This provides great flexibility, but the size limits in any rail vehicle mean that power is developed in a relatively wasteful manner, especially with a steam engine. In the early days of steam, Isambard Kingdom Brunel tried to marry the advantages of the railway train with the benefits of a central power station using the atmospheric system. Alas the technology was not adequate, and the venture failed. By the 1850s, a few visionaries were proclaiming electric traction as the future of railways, but until the problems of reliable compact motors, effective power transmission over reasonable distances, and how power should be picked up were solved, the electric railway was a dream, and nothing more. The first practical electric locomotive in the world was exhibited by Werner von Siemens (1816-1892) at the Berlin Trades Exhibition in 1879. It was a tiny four wheel box on which the driver sat, and it ran up and down a short length of track. It was little more than a novelty, but it demonstrated that an electric vehicle could run on power supplied from a stationary plant of some sort. The problems of transmitting power over any distance meant that the most suitable application for electric traction was in replacing horse or steam trams in the streets, and within two years, the first electric tramway had appeared. The first electric railways in Britain, the Giant's Causeway Tramway in Ulster and the Volks Electric Railway at Brighton followed in 1883. In 1890, the City & South London railway opened. It was the first deep tube railway in the world, and initially used four wheel electric locomotives. In 1898, the Waterloo & City Railway was opened, connecting Waterloo with the heart of the business district in the City of London. The first main line surface electrification of an existing railway was carried out by the Lancashire & Yorkshire Railway between Liverpool and Southport in 1904. Within a few years a bewildering array of third rail and overhead systems had evolved. Over the years, most fell by the wayside, until just two alternative methods triumphed, 750v DC third rail and 25 kv ac overhead power supply. In this section we will look at the early designs, some of the systems that fell by the wayside, and DC and AC stock built up to 1960.

Above: Magnus Volk (1851-1937) was the son of a clock maker, and lived in Brighton. He was a gifted innovator, and at the start of the 1880s was installing electric street fire alarms, telephones and a public lighting system in Brighton. One offshoot of this was the construction of a short electric railway to two-

foot gauge. It ran along the seafront, and was opened by the Mayor of Brighton in August 1883. Because the Giant's Causeway Railway in Ireland had carried out its first trial runs earlier in 1883, and because the Volk's Railway was rebuilt to a different gauge after its first season, protagonists of the two systems still dispute who is entitled to premier place. In its rebuilt form, Volk's Electric Railway was extended and altered to the unusual gauge of 2 ft 8 ins. In its original form, the current was conducted via the rails rather than via a live rail, but for the 1884 re-opening, a live third rail was laid. This was slightly off-centre between the running rails. Sadly the original 1883 car was broken up in 1939, and all the stock now on the railway dates from 1890 or later. Passengers put their feet up on the dashboard of No 3, as a two car set heads along the seafront on a glorious summer day in 1994.

Opposite page, top: Despite the success of the Volks' railway and a few other lines, electric traction was still a novelty in the late 1880s, and when parliamentary approval was sought by the Glasgow District Subway Company for a 6½ mile railway, cable traction was envisaged. The subway comprised two parallel tubes that followed a circular course, crossing under the Clyde twice, and cars worked in a clockwise or anticlockwise direction. There were no points on either circle, cars being craned to the car shed which was at surface level. Another unusual feature was the gauge of four feet. The line opened on 14th December 1896. The subway worked in the same way as a cable tramway, with a continuous cable for each track, powered from a steam generating station. The cable ran continuously during the hours of operation, and gripper cars were provided with a vice like grip that the gripman closed on to the cable to start the car. At a station, he released the grip, allowing the car to lose momentum, and then applied the brakes. The rolling stock consisted of bogie grip cars and

four-wheel trailers, which were later rebuilt as bogie stock. In 1922, the Subway was bought by Glasgow Corporation. By then, it was showing signs of age, and electrification was considered. The line was converted in 1935, the old grip cars becoming motor cars and receiving new underframes. The cars, which were only ever seen on one side by the public, had doors on that side only. Originally they had been painted red and cream on the public side and drab maroon on the offside, but the public side changed to red in 1954. Except for electrification, the subway continued little changed from Victorian days until the 1970s, by which time the condition of the tunnels was giving cause for alarm. Modernisation was agreed, and the old subway was scheduled to close for rebuilding on 29th May 1977. In the event, the discovery of cracks in the tunnel wall near Govan Cross caused a precipitate closure just after 1.00pm on 21st May 1977. This view at Bridge Street was taken just after services had ended, and captures set 17, comprising cars 43 and 11 on the inner circle, and set 7 with power car No 20 on the outer circle.

Opposite page, bottom : The subway cars were designed by D Home Morton. Except for the replacement of the original longitudinal mahogany and birch stripwood seats by leather seats, and the installation of fluorescent lighting in the 1960s, the interior of Motor car No 11 had changed little since it had been built by the Oldbury Carriage & Wagon Co of Birmingham in 1896. Capable of seating 42 passengers, the wide aisle permitted much higher loads at peak periods. Trailer car No 43 in the distance has retained the original style of battened wooden floor without hatches, whilst No 11 has a floor covered in linoleum with hatches giving access to the power bogies. Although the power cars came from Oldbury in 1896, trailer 43 came from Hurst Nelson & Co of Motherwell in 1898.

Below left: By the early 1890s, the London & South Western Railway was taking an ever-greater number of businessmen to and from the City each day. When they left Waterloo station, they were still some distance from the city, and a nominally independent company was formed by the LSWR to build the Waterloo & City Railway. It was to be the only deep tube line owned by a main line railway company. Construction of the 12-foot diameter tube began in 1894, and the line was formally opened in July 1898, public services commencing on 8th August 1898. Four-car multiple unit sets were provided by Jackson & Sharp of Wilmington, Delaware, and single cars for off-peak services came from Dick, Kerr & Co of Preston. No 15 was one of five British-built double-ended cars dating from 1899. The Dick Kerr cars closely followed the body design of the American-built multiple units. With growing traffic, more stock came in 1904 and 1922, and survived until 1940.

Below right: In 1904, the Lancashire & Yorkshire Railway opened the first section of what was to become a network of 650v DC electrified lines on Merseyside. The first section was between Liverpool Exchange station and the popular residential town and resort of Southport. Electrification would also permit a great increase in terminal capacity at Liverpool Exchange, saving costly enlargement, 'by using motor car trains instead of locomotives, you double the capacity of your terminal accommodation'. The decision was taken on 22nd October 1902, and the first trial trip ran on 29th December 1903. The full public service commenced on 13th May 1904. The cars were jointly produced by the LYR Horwich works and Dick, Kerr & Co, and were 60 feet long, and to the exceptional width of 10 feet. The line from Liverpool to Aintree, home of the 'Grand National' was electrified in 1906, and electric trains reached Ormskirk in 1911.

Aspinall was very pleased with the results, and commented, 'this experience has convinced me that there are a number of suburban lines round our great cities, and especially near London, which can be electrified with advantage to the public and to the railway companies, though we must wait awhile before dealing with long distance travelling'.

Bottom: When the City & South London Railway was electrified in 1890, it was the first deep level tube in the world. Within 15 years, the cut and cover Metropolitan and Metropolitan District railways had been electrified, and several new deep tube lines had been built. An American tycoon, Charles Tyson Yerkes, (1837-1905) was behind much of the progress in the early 1900s. His business methods were hardly scrupulous, and he had been virtually run out of town in Chicago in 1899, but he got things done fast. One result was to create the Underground Group which included the District Railway, and most of the deep tube lines. This included the Great Northern, Piccadilly & Brompton, which opened in December 1906. Willing to buy equipment from the States, France, Germany and even Hungary, the Yerkes lines created stock with a family resemblance that owed little to earlier British traditions. The GNP&B stock came from Les Ateliers du Construction du Nord de la France at Valenciennes, and the Hungarian Railway Carriage & Wagon works at Raab. This study of driving power car No 9 recalls the combination of a clerestory roof, tall end doors, a frame bowed up over the power bogie, massive louvres above the power bogie, and a low slung passenger section that set the shape of tube stock for the next twenty years. Passenger access was via hand operated lattice doors at the far end of the car. Largely displaced by the 1923 and 1938 stock, the last two cars survived until 1956.

Right: The mixture of longitudinal and transverse seating and hand straps for standing passengers in rush hour set a pattern that would be familiar to London commuters almost a century later. This interior scene, and the previous view are from a range of 1906 colour postcards produced for the various companies within the Underground Group to publicise the opening of no less than three lines, the Baker Street & Waterloo (colloquially the Bakerloo Line) which opened in March 1906, GNP&B, which became known as the Piccadilly Line, and finally the Charing Cross, Euston & Hampstead which was fully opened in 1907. In less than 20 years, between 1890 and 1910, the core of the present London Underground system was either electrified, or built from scratch. It was an astonishing achievement, and as with the speed of the LYR electrification, something we could not come close to emulating today. As in so much else, the debt we owe to our Victorian and Edwardian forebears is immense.

Below: To understand the conflict that arose between the proponents of low voltage DC third rail systems and high voltage ac overhead systems in the early 1900s, we must look at the theory of electric power transmission. The main drawback of low voltage DC systems is that power loss is severe even over short distances, and three miles has always been regarded as a long distance to transmit low voltage DC current. In the early days this was no great hardship as early DC power stations were small and located at frequent intervals. By 1903 technology had advanced and high voltage AC power stations were feasible. Power could be transmitted via high tension AC feeders to local sub-stations, where it would be transformed down to line voltage and converted to DC, but

this required a great deal of local plant. It was cheaper to provide a high tension supply to the trains themselves, but most engineers felt that this necessitated an overhead power supply. The Midland Railway electrified the short section from Morecambe and Heysham to Lancaster in 1908. It was intended as a test bed for possible future developments, and 21 miles of track were electrified, using a 6,600v 25 Hz single-phase system developed by AEG of Germany. The London, Brighton & South Coast Railway had obtained powers as early as 1903 to electrify its suburban lines south of the Thames. The eminent electrical engineer, Sir Phillip Dawson, was appointed to supervise the project, and AEG of Berlin, the British Thompson Houston Co, and Siemens were involved in the contract. The 'Elevated Electric'

as it was known covered the routes from London Bridge to Peckham Rye, Battersea Park and Victoria, and scheduled services began on 1st December 1909. The same 6.6kv 25 Hz system as adopted on the Midland was chosen, and further extensions followed in 1911. The LBSCR even considered extending electric services to Brighton itself, but the outbreak of war in 1914, and inevitable break with the German suppliers, spelled the demise of the project. In this portrait, we are looking at an Elevated Electric three-car set, with a First Class Trailer between two Third Class Motor Driving cars. The LBSCR was at the cutting edge of railway electrification, with a state of the art AC overhead electric system.

Above: In the early 1900s, there were two seemingly contradictory trends in commuter traffic in the London area. Short rail journeys in the vicinity of the newly electrified London tram routes plummeted, causing a serious fall in the revenue of lines such as the North London Railway that relied heavily on such traffic. On the other hand, where longer distances were involved, for example to Watford, traffic increased. As early as 1907, the LNWR considered electrifying its suburban services to Watford, but unlike other schemes, where electrification had been to obviate the need for additional lines, the LNWR plan included a new electrified suburban line. After many years of close association with the NLR, the LNWR took over day-to-day control of the North London in 1909. Tackling NLR problems became urgent, and a plan was agreed in 1911. A new suburban line was to start near Euston. It would run alongside the existing main lines towards Watford, but just short of Watford Junction,

would diverge into the centre of town, with a branch serving Croxley Green as well. The NLR lines from their city terminus at Broad Street would be electrified to Dalston Junction and then westwards to Camden and Willesden where connections were made with the LNWR, whilst the line from Willesden Junction to Richmond would also be electrified. The new suburban lines out to Watford (which are still known to railwaymen as the New Line) were opened in 1912-13, but electric services did not commence until 1914, and further progress was delayed by the outbreak of war. Further extensions took place in 1916-17, but it was not until 1922 that the scheme was completed. The first four sets of 1914 used Siemens' equipment, but the remaining stock built from 1915 to 1923 used electrical equipment by the Oerlikon company of Switzerland. Bodywork came from Metropolitan Carriage Wagon & Finance Co of Saltley, or from Wolverton. Driving Motor Third M28262 was one of the original 1915 Oerlikon

cars, and had been delivered as LNWR 43E as a Spare Motor car, for use in sets when the set's own Motor car was stopped for attention. The body came from Metropolitan at Saltley. The far car, M29027M is a 1915 Control (or Driving) trailer, built at Wolverton and originally numbered 307E. A few Oerlikon cars had been scrapped as a result of damage, but it was only when new BR stock was ordered for delivery from 1957 onwards, that withdrawal of the Oerlikon sets began in earnest. The last public run by an Oerlikon set was in April 1960, but one set was retained for shunting at Stonebridge Park depot, and another pair of cars, M28262M and M29027M, were retained as the Chief Electrical Engineer's test set. It was stabled at Mitre Bridge for some time, but by August 1969 was lying out of service at the disused Locomotive Testing Station at Rugby.

Opposite page, below: After the end of the First World War, the Underground Group decided to replace the first generation tube stock dating back to the 1890s and early1900s. For the tube lines, a new clerestory roofed design was developed for use throughout the system. Although fitted with power operated sliding doors, rather than the hand worked lattice gates that had characterised the 1906-07 stock on the Piccadilly and Bakerloo lines, the new Standard stock, as it was known, was descended from the older designs with a similar roof profile, end and side doors to the driving compartments, and the frame swept up over the power bogie. The stock was built by various makers with a myriad of design differences from 1923 to 1930. Further cars for the Piccadilly line extensions were built in 1931-34. With a large control compartment behind the driver, the seating capacity of the motor cars was only 30, compared to 44/48 of the trailer cars. The appearance of the 1938 stock led to a new name for the old Standard cars. They were now called 1923 stock or pre-1938 stock. Forty years after they first appeared, the 1923 cars were still in use on the Central, Piccadilly and Northern lines, but by 1966 they had reached the end of the road as far as LT was concerned. A few cars exchanged the tunnels beneath London for the

fields of the Isle of Wight, and were even to be lashed by the waters of the Solent on winter nights. The steam era was drawing to a close on the island, but no standard BR stock was small enough for the cramped confines of Ryde tunnel, so 43 Standard cars were transferred to the island in 1966-67 prior to the introduction of electrified services on 20th March 1967. At first marshalled as 4-VEC and 3-TIS sets, their designation coming from the Roman name for the island, Vectis, they were altered to 5-VEC and 2-TIS sets in 1985. 5-VEC set 485-044 heads through Ryde St John's station towards Ryde Pier Head in 1987. The nearest car, No 7, had once been LT 3209. The end came for these veterans in 1991, and their replacements were cascaded 1938 tube cars.

Above: In the early 1900s, the Great Central Railway started to build a deep-water harbour at Immingham, some miles along the coast from the important fishing port of Grimsby. A contractor's railway was upgraded for passenger service in 1910, using a steam railcar. In 1912 this was replaced by the Grimsby & Immingham Light Railway. This was an interurban electric line of the type familiar in the United States, but rare in Britain, the most notable examples being at Immingham and in the Isle of Man. Single

deck bogie cars were built to carry workmen to the docks and industries that developed in the area. With increasing traffic after the Second World War, some second-hand Newcastle trams were acquired, and in 1951, nineteen more cars came from Gateshead. They became Nos 17-33 on the Grimsby & Immingham. They had been built between 1923 and 1928 by Brush, or at Gateshead. After the closure of the Grimsby & Immingham, Gateshead No 5, by then carrying British Railways electric stock dark green livery as No 20, went to the National Tramway Museum at Crich. When photographed at Crich on 24th July 1964, it was still in BR colours, but was subsequently restored to Gateshead livery as No 5.

Above: By the 1920s, there was a bewildering array of different electrification systems. The Southern had inherited the 6.6 kv Brighton Elevated electric and the 600v DC third rail system instituted by the LSWR. The ex-LSWR men had a key voice on the Southern, and that, plus the greater extent of the third rail system, sealed the fate of the Brighton Elevated. The LMS inherited the 630v DC third rail lines in North London, 6.6 kv overhead on the Midland at Morecambe, the LYR 630v DC network around Liverpool, and a 1,200v DC section from Manchester to Bury. This was also built by the LYR, and used a unique shielded high voltage third rail. The LNER had taken over the 600v DC Tyneside electric lines, and a freight-only 1,500v DC overhead system at Shildon. Although each section was isolated, and there was no immediate prospect of through running, the multiplication of different power systems would cause problems when electrification did spread. In time-honoured tradition, two committees were set up, and reported decisively in favour of 1,500v DC overhead electrification. At the time the only line in the British Isles using this system was the Newport-Shildon freight line, which was closed in 1935 as falling traffic meant that services could be more economically worked by steam. At the time the committees were deliberating, the LMS and LNER were planning to electrify the jointly owned Manchester, South Junction & Altrincham Railway, which ran south west from Manchester (London Road) station (later known as Piccadilly) for nine miles. It was a very busy suburban route, and the parent companies agreed to adopt the new national standard. Electric services began on 11th May 1931. Metropolitan Cammell Carriage & Wagon Co provided 22 three car sets, together with two spare motor coaches. Before the war they were numbered in a separate series, but early in BR days were included in the LM series numbering system. M28587M was a Driving Motor Brake Third, and is seen at the car depot at Altrincham on 27th April 1971. At the time I was studying for my law finals at university, and my revision included a visit to Altrincham on a day that I had no lectures, to photograph the Altrincham sets before services ended on 30th April 1971. Happily I got the photos and my degree. The line was converted for 25 kv operation, and class 304 units replaced the elderly Altrincham sets. Although the new sets had a higher top speed that the old cars, they did not have the same acceleration, and with the close spacing of stations of the MSJ&AR, the result was a slower journey time!

Opposite page, bottom: The Southern had expanded the LSWR three rail system dramatically, and had replaced the technically superior but smaller 'Brighton Elevated' electric with the three-rail system in the late 1920s. In 1929, with the Great Depression at its height and Winston Churchill as Chancellor of the Exchequer, the government repealed the Railway Passenger Duty, an absurd tax on rail passengers, on condition that the railways used the savings on projects that would ease unemployment. The Southern decided to inaugurate the first trunk route electrification in Britain, by extending the third rail all the way to Brighton. Electric services commenced on 1st January 1933. The Brighton line was host to one of the most legendary trains in Britain, the Pullman car train, *The Southern Belle*. The last steam Belle ran on 31st December 1932, and the three five-car sets which were built for what was to become the *Brighton Belle* were the first electric Pullman trains in the world. They were ordered by the Pullman Car Co, and classed 5-BEL under the SR electric stock classification system. They were built by Metropolitan-Cammell, and consisted of a Motor Brake Third, a Third Parlour car, two First Class cars and another Motor Brake Third. The set was 335 feet long, weighed 249 tons, and seated 40 First and 152 Third class passengers. The 5-BEL sets entered service as 2051-2053, but were renumbered 3051-3053 in January 1937. Set 2051(3051) consisted of Motor Car 88, Firsts *Hazel* and *Doris*, Third Parlour Car 86 and Motor Car 89. Famous passengers to use the

train included Oliver Bulleid and Sir Laurence Olivier, who was particularly partial to the superb grilled kippers served on the Belle. A 1969 decision to abandon kippers led to a formidable outcry and reinstatement of kippers, but sadly the Belle was taken off on Sunday 30th April 1972.

Bottom: There can be few more spectacular vantage points from which to watch trains than the twelfth century keep, which lies in the V of the famous diamond crossing at the east end of Newcastle station. Newcastle had electrified its trams as early as December 1901, and within two years, the North Eastern Railway had lost 40% of its suburban traffic in the area. The first section of the Tyneside electric system to Tynemouth came into use in 1904. By 1917, 37 route miles were electrified and suburban traffic had recovered to pre tramway levels. Between 1934 and 1938, the LNER electrified the South Tyneside lines to South Shields. Most of the NER stock was replaced in 1937 by 64 twin-car articulated sets. Four different types of set were produced, with different amounts of First and Third class accommodation and provision for luggage. Trains, which could consist of up to four two-car sections, were carefully made up to reflect traffic needs. The cars were built to Gresley's specification by Metropolitan-Cammell, with electrical equipment from Westinghouse, and electric motors by Crompton Parkinson. At the time of their withdrawal, they were the last Gresley articulated stock in passenger service. At the

time of this 1967 view, the Tyneside electric sets were working out their last weeks of service, as BR had taken a decision to end electric operation and replace the smooth quiet and efficient EMUs by diesel multiple units. It was a controversial and unpopular decision, and within a few years electric traction had returned with the Tyne & Wear Metro.

Left: The 1930s saw many fine new designs of electric stock, and the formation of London Transport in 1933 heralded further changes. The 1923 Standard stock, with its long control cabinets, was now outmoded, and the Chief Mechanical Engineer, W S Graff-Baker believed that it was now possible to mount the control equipment below floor level. Some experimental cars with streamlined ends appeared in 1935/36. Though dramatic, the streamlined ends did not offer much benefit for London conditions, but the cars did confirm Graff-Baker's ideas over equipment, and the 1938 stock, in which the full length of the saloon, save for a short driving cab, was available for passengers, marked a big step forward. Over 1100 cars were delivered between June 1938 and the outbreak of war in September 1939. A Bakerloo line 1938 Tube stock set is seen in platform 3 at Willesden Junction on 12th August 1979. The LNWR station buildings and signal box, *Willesden New Station*, reveal that this section was built as a part of the LNWR electrification project, and included joint operation of Underground and LNWR stock. The sheer quantity of railway infrastructure in this area is remarkable.

Opposite page, bottom: The Mersey Railway opened the first tunnel between Liverpool and Birkenhead in 1886. It was steam worked, but until electrification at 650v DC in 1903, it was not popular with passengers. It made an end-on junction at Birkenhead Park station with the Wirral Railway, and at Rock Ferry shared a station with the Birkenhead Joint Railway (LNWR & GWR). The Wirral railway was not electrified in 1903, so passengers from the Wirral towns to Liverpool faced the inconvenience of changing trains in what might be a 5 or 6 mile ride. It was not until 1938, fifteen years after the Wirral railway became part of the LMS, that it was finally electrified. LMS trains now worked over the Mersey Railway into Liverpool, and Mersey trains worked out to New Brighton. This curious partnership between the vast LMS and the tiny but fiercely independent Mersey Railway continued until 1948, when the Mersey railway was absorbed into BR. The LMS ordered 19 three-car sets from Metropolitan-Cammell for electrification in 1938. As through running over the Mersey was an integral part of the scheme, they had to conform to the 650v Mersey supply. These Stanier electric sets were of all metal construction, using high strength alloys, much of the strength coming from the body shell. Centre couplers were used, and as the sets would not operate with ordinary stock,

they were not fitted with conventional buffers. In 1958, another 24 sets were built to the same design to replace the original Mersey Railway stock. M28681M is one of the original LMS built Driving Motor Thirds, and is seen at Birkenhead North en route to Liverpool in the late 1970s. The all-over rail blue colour scheme represented the nadir of rolling stock liveries. It wore badly, weathered badly, and looked depressing even on a sunny day. In the 1970s and 80s a massive reorganisation of the suburban lines took place on Merseyside, and the LMS designed electric sets on the Wirral were replaced in the mid-1980s with the 1979 built class 508 units which had been built for Merseyside, but diverted to the Southern region for some years.

Top: With the Wirral electrification completed, the LMS turned its attention to the former LYR electric services to Southport, Aintree and Ormskirk. The original LYR stock of 1904 was still in service, and in 1939, deliveries began of 59 Driving Motor Cars, 59 Driving Trailers and 34 Non-Driving Trailers. Owing to the outbreak of war, the order was not completed until 1943. Electrical equipment came from English Electric, and the firm was so proud of the cars that they appeared in the English Electric Traction brochures for years, along with the

claim, 'one of the motor coaches ran for two years without any attention being necessary to the control equipment, which was sealed up during this period'. Originally in LMS crimson lake, the sets carried the various shades of BR electric stock green until the 1960s, when they received the same drab all-over blue that the Wirral sets carried. They were replaced in the late 1970s by the class 507 sets. At Southport, there was a triangular junction just outside the station with lines radiating to Liverpool and to Preston and Wigan. Short sections of the Preston and Wigan lines were electrified in 1909. M29865M, in EMU green, approaches Southport station with a working from the Crossens/Meols Cop triangle on 22nd July 1964, a few months before the Meols Cop and Crossens electric services ended, leaving just the Liverpool route electrified. This car had started life as a Third Composite Trailer, No 29820, but had been rebuilt as a Driving Trailer Composite after the war.

Top: On the Southern Railway, Oliver Bulleid had directed his considerable talents to improving the dated look of its electric trains. As early as February 1939, reference was made to a proposed new curved sided all welded suburban set which would accommodate six passengers aside. The first 4-SUB set did not appear until 1941, a second prototype was completed later, and a further eight just before the end of the war. Welded construction and curved sides permitted six-aside seating, yet kept the stock within the loading gauge. Construction began in earnest after the end of hostilities, and the design was adopted as the basis of the British Railways 4-EPB. The main differences were electro-pneumatic brakes and improved performance. Introduced in 1951, the 4-EPB, later class 415/1, became a familiar sight on Southern Region suburban services to

generations of commuters. Indeed it is likely that up to three generations may have commuted to work on the same vehicles! A refurbishment programme began as late as 1979, the overhauled sets being designated 415/4. Forty years after they had first been introduced, and fifty years after the appearance of the prototype Bulleid car, my father photographed 5170 at the newly redeveloped Charing Cross station. It was one of the last railway photographs he took before he passed away later in 1991. In the 1990s, the 4-EPBs finally bowed out, as a new generation of stock replaced them, but two sets, 5001 and 5176 were still in store awaiting disposal at the start of 1999 sixty years after work began on the pioneer Bulleid design! As with I K Brunel or F W Webb, Bulleid is criticised for some of his design foibles, or ideas that went awry. All three

were brilliant engineers who dared to innovate, rather than play safe. Some things did go wrong, but that was the price of their success.

Below left: In the mid-thirties, the LNER started electrifying the suburban lines from Liverpool Street station to Shenfield, and from Manchester (London Rd) to Sheffield. These were the most ambitious electrification programmes yet. In accordance with the Pringle and Weir reports which had recommended 1500 v DC overhead electrification as the national standard, both were to be built to this system. Work ceased when war broke out, but was resumed after the war, although neither scheme was ready before nationalisation. The Shenfield electrification came into use in 1949, but the Manchester-Sheffield service did not begin until 1954. The stock supplied for the Shenfield electrification had been ordered as far back as 1938, but placed on hold, and the design revised by Arthur Peppercorn, the last CME of the LNER and Mechanical Engineer to the Eastern and North Eastern regions of BR until his retirement in 1949. Construction of the Glossop cars followed on as soon as the Shenfield stock had been completed, and the vehicles were placed in store until required. They were built by Metropolitan Cammell and Birmingham Railway Carriage & Wagon Co, and both designs were very similar. GEC motors of a slightly lower power output than the Crompton Parkinson equipment on the Shenfield sets was used, and this led to problems when the sets were tried on the long climb to Penistone. As a result, they spent their career on the Manchester-Hadfield-Glossop section. Driving Trailer Second M59604 pauses at Gorton station on a dismal day in December 1972.

Right: The 2-HAP units, later class 414, were built for the Kent Coast and South coast dormitory towns services. These required semi-fast workings with lavatory accommodation, but higher density seating than was common on long distance sets. 173 units were built between 1957 and 1959. The leading set in this unit is 6014, one of the first sets to be built. Problems with the riding characteristics led to the introduction of Commonwealth bogies at the inner ends of the later sets. 6014 is entering Deal on 8th June 1973. In 1974, many units, including 6014, were downgraded to all Second, and reclassified 2-SAP. The inverted black triangle was to inform station staff that the luggage accommodation was located at this end of the set. In common with much stock built at this period, the 2-HAP sets were insulated with asbestos, and whilst some sets had been rebuilt and the asbestos lagging removed, a Health and Safety edict laid down that any sets which retained asbestos would have to be taken out of service by the end of 1987. In general the Southern EMUs shared the same body characteristics as the Mk I steam hauled stock, and superb though this was, there were a number of accidents involving first generation stock where there was some telescoping. The most serious accident was at Clapham Junction in 1988. It prompted media frenzy about old stock, and demands by the Health and Safety Executive that such stock should be taken out of service. The current rules, enshrined in the Railway Safety Regulations of 1999, make it illegal to operate Mk I bodied stock in passenger service after 1st January 2003, unless it has been fitted with an anti-override device. This will affect approximately 1,000 vehicles, which are the last survivors of the Mk I family. J G Robinson of the GCR had developed a saw-toothed device just before the First World War to lock carriages together in case of a collision. It was fitted to many GC coaches but was never tested in earnest. Railway officers of the day

pointed out that it would add to the mass and hence the destructive power of stock, and would be useless unless both vehicles that collided were so fitted. The system demanded by the H&SE of today is a cup and cone mounted on the headstocks of vehicles in place of traditional buffers. At least one senior railway engineer has pointed out that the new system will only be effective if two Mk Is collide with one another. It is uncanny how history so often repeats itself.

Below: In the 1930s, the LMS drew up ambitious plans to rebuild Euston, and extend the former North Western electric services, which would receive new stock with power operated sliding doors, as on the Wirral and Southport sections. War intervened, and it was not until 1955 that BR placed orders for replacement stock for the veteran LNWR North London sets on the Euston-Watford and Broad St-Richmond services. Electrical equipment and traction motors were by GEC, with four 185 hp motors in each power car. The new sets, on a short 57-foot underframe, due to clearance problems, were basically a three-car version of

the standard Southern Region suburban set, but with the ends modified to accept a service number panel and a destination blind. Because of tight clearances in Hampstead Heath tunnel, they were fitted with bars on the window droplights. The first of 57 sets entered public service on 27th May 1957, and more sets arrived throughout the year. Then an interval of several months ensued whilst the new stock was run in, and enough of the Oerlikon sets were retained to cover any troubles. Only in August 1958 did commissioning resume, and it was not until October 1959 that the last set entered traffic. Motor Open Brake Second M61159 is the nearest vehicle in this set running on the multiple track approaches to Euston on 25th June 1974. The B1 code indicates that it is an ordinary passenger train (B) and that it is on a Euston-Watford service (1). Code C was used for ECS, and numbers 2-9 for other routes. A second letter, O, X, Y, or Z indicated a depot working, so that a Broad St-Mitre Bridge empty set would be coded CO. Classed 501 by BR, they were eventually replaced by class 313 units from the former GNR section.

Above: The channel ports suffered special operating problems, as the railways had to deal with large crowds moving with lots of luggage. In steam days, adding an extra bogie van on the set was the answer. This could be shunted down the quay lines to the vicinity of the ship. Electrification ruled that out, as it was unsafe to electrify the quay lines at Dover or Folkestone. The Southern Region came up with a solution, in a three rail/battery Motor Luggage Van. Ten MLVs were introduced in 1959, the design resembling a Mk I BG with 2-HAP ends, which is just what it was. The MLV had cabs at each end, so could be coupled to a passenger set, such as a 4-CEP, and work as a normal Driving Motor Coach, but on arrival at the port, it could uncouple and run under battery power along the quay lines. The main drawback was that they could only run for about 20 minutes under battery power before returning to the live rail section. Later designated class 419, MLV 68008 is the rear vehicle as a heavy boat train starts up the sharply curved climb from Folkestone Harbour station on 8th June 1973. The first two cars, 68001-002 were built at Eastleigh under Lot 30458 in 1959, and the remaining eight under Lot 30623 in 1960-61. No fewer than eight of these cars survived in the Porterbrook leasing fleet as Class 931 tractor units in 1999, 68008 having become 931 098.

Left: By the mid-fifties, the original LYR electric sets on the Manchester-Bury route needed replacement. This line was third rail, but worked to the exceptionally high figure of 1200v DC. Because of the hazard this posed, the third rail was cased in wood. Electric pickup was by sideways contact. The voltage and collection system would have made the new sets unique, but the riding of the first generation BR electric stock had caused concern, and as a stopgap, an electrified version of the Gresley bogie was developed for the Bury sets. Criticisms of the slab-fronted appearance of early BR electric units prompted a more stylish sloping front, and the new stock entered service in 1959. Motor Open Brake Second M65461 enters Heaton Park station in the last few days of operation of the Manchester-Bury electrics in 1991. The car carries the Greater Manchester orange and brown livery. The line was rebuilt as a part of the Greater Manchester Metrolink, using Firema six-axle articulated supertrams.

Right: The Manchester-Sheffield electrification of 1954 was the swansong of the 1500v DC system advocated in the Weir and Pringle reports of the 1920s. R A Riddles had been critical of 1500v DC, believing that 25kv AC was far superior, as it would offer considerable savings in sub-station equipment, a lighter overhead construction, as a higher voltage reduces the current required, and it is high currents that require heavy line wires. The down side was that the engineers originally calculated a 23 inch minimum overhead clearance if 25 kv were to be used, to obviate the risk of flashovers. If the voltage were reduced to 6.25kv, the gap could be reduced to 11 inches. A dual voltage system was therefore adopted, 6.25kv in urban areas where there were many bridges, and 25 kv out in the country. Once the Eastern Region's Liverpool Street to Southend routes had been electrified, there was pressure to electrify the Fenchurch Street to Shoeburyness line. Construction of what became known as the 'LTS' stock began in 1958, and by 1959, some were in temporary service on the Colchester and Clacton routes. By 1961, the LTS sets had gained a very bad reputation after their transfer to the Tilbury section. One of the railway inspecting officers, Brigadier Langley, investigated, and placed much of the blame on the change over between 6.25 kv and 25 kv. This was cured, but brought the dual voltage concept into doubt, and heralded the eventual demise of the 6.25 kv inner urban system. No 302 266 powers south through Whittlesford on the GE Liverpool St to Cambridge line in July 1987.

Below: The late 1950s saw an ambitious scheme to modernise the suburban services along the banks of the Clyde. Lines radiating from Glasgow along the north and south banks of the river were to be electrified at 25 kv, and would receive a radically new design of stock. Garbed in an eye-catching Caledonian blue, the blue trains', as they were known, were built by Pressed Steel Co of Paisley, and a dramatic new front with wrap round windows was developed by the newly formed BR Design Panel. The first cars were completed in May 1959, but by December 1960, the entire class was in disgrace, and steam trains were running once more! There had been two serious explosions on board. Eventually these were traced to an equipment compartment that contained low-tension switchgear and a reservoir for the oil used as coolant for the onboard transformers. A potentially explosive air-gas mixture built up in the closed compartment, and was ignited by the switchgear operation. The wrap round windscreen was also troublesome. It was prone to leakage and expensive to replace, and a smaller flat screen was later provided. Set 303 045 leaves Glasgow Central for Hamilton in the late 1970s.

A PRIDE OF PULLMANS

When I was a child, my parents sometimes holidayed in the New Forest. Roaming in the woods, or playing on the beach were fun, but the real treat was to watch Oliver Bulleid's magnificent 'Merchant Navy' class pacifics thunder through Brockenhurst on the *Bournemouth Belle*, or see them depart from Bournemouth itself, wheels flailing round in the characteristic Bulleid slip. Then I started to discover Pullman cars in other places, such as the East Coast main line, and one day my father and I discovered a grounded Pullman car body dating back to the 1870s. In a book on coaching stock, I decided that there could be no finer way to bring the colour section to a close than with a nostalgic look at the wonderful legacy of George Mortimer Pullman. In deciding the title for this section, I wondered what the collective noun for Pullman cars should be. If pride is the proper collective word for that most majestic beast, the lion, it surely applies to the Pullman as well.

Right: Known to Pullman staff as, 'the coat of arms', this was the second Pullman device, and appeared on the 1960 cars, and older stock as they were repainted. It embraced the heraldic arms of England, Scotland, Ireland and Wales, and was emblazoned twice on the side of each car, until the ill-judged decision to adopt rail blue and grey after the Pullman service was finally merged into BR mainstream operations.

Below right: Pullman was born in 1831, and legend has it that he was so disgusted after travelling on an American overnight train that he decided to create a luxury sleeping car service. His first car appeared in 1858, but it was not until 1865 that the business took off in America. In 1872, Sir James Allport, General Manager of the Midland Railway, visited America. He was impressed by the Pullman cars, and invited Pullman to visit England. A 15-year contract was signed with the MR, and the first American-built Pullman sleeping cars were shipped over in sections and assembled at the MR works at Derby. The first Pullman train ran on 1st June 1874. Pullman cars commenced on the LBSCR in 1875 and on the Great Northern in 1879. My parents served in North Africa and Italy during the war, and later at Lincoln Military Hospital. They had fond memories of the town, and on one visit to there on 16th October 1965, my father and I looked round Lincoln St Marks, the old Midland station. We found this grounded American-built 1870s Pullman car, and assumed we had discovered one of the early Midland cars. Later, I found out more about the car we had photographed. It was *Iona*, and had been assembled at the Pullman car shops at Derby in 1880 from parts supplied from the Pullman Palace Car Company works in Detroit, but it was for the GNR, not for the Midland. Pullman services had started on the GNR the previous year, but *Iona* and a sister

car, *Columba* were the first new Pullman sleeping cars on the GN. Operating for a while as East Coast Joint Stock, *Iona* was renumbered GNR No 2992 in 1901, and converted into a dining car. Although Pullman was renowned for sleeping car services in America and the earliest British Pullmans were sleepers, the change from sleeper to dining car was symbolic of the Pullman business in England. Thought to have run on the Nottingham-Skegness line, No 2992 outlived all her contemporaries in service, and was not withdrawn until October 1925. *Iona* was taken to Lincoln and grounded for use by the Mutual Improvement class at the GN shed, the shed being quite close to the *Midland* station in the town! Sadly this wonderful old car was broken up c1970. Happily some of the contemporary first generation Midland cars that were also grounded, have survived into preservation.

Opposite page, top: George M Pullman died in 1897, but the US company continued to operate in England for another decade. During this period, more American built Pullman cars came to Britain, but in 1907, D A Dalziel, later Lord Dalziel (1854-1927), purchased the British operation. Henceforth new cars were built in

England. The oldest surviving British car is *Emerald*, a type K car of 1910. In Pullman parlance, 'K' meant an open saloon car with kitchen. It was schedule number 32 in the Pullman car list and was built by the Birmingham Carriage & Wagon Co, for services on the SE&CR. It was taken out of service after fire damage, and used as a training car from 1955 to 1963. In 1960, a large batch of new Pullman cars, based on the Mk I body shell, entered service, permitting wholesale withdrawal of older cars, some of which had seen 40 or 50 years of service. It is often said that *Emerald* went to Betws-y-Coed as a Camping Coach in May 1960, but in fact it was a 1921 car, *Anaconda* (Pullman list No 132, BR camping coach No 022260) that went there. This car was not in the best condition, and was replaced in 1964 by *Emerald*. (BR camping coach No 021803). It is an easy mistake to make, as both cars were similar, the most obvious difference being the buffers, round on the first car, elliptical on *Emerald*. She is seen whilst in use at Betws-y-Coed on 8th August 1971, but now forms part of the Conwy Valley Railway Museum.

Above: The oldest operable Pullman is type P car No 59 *Topaz*, of 1914. 'P' stood for parlour, a term reflecting the American ancestry of the Pullman company. The English definition would be open or saloon. This car also came from Birmingham C & W, and went to the SE&CR. It was withdrawn in 1960, and set aside for preservation at the Clapham Museum of Transport. After closure of the Clapham museum, it went to the NRM at York. Although Pullman did not invent sleeping cars or railway catering cars, he popularised both and developed them. Very basic on-board catering had existed in Britain before Pullman, but the start of Pullman services on the GNR in 1879 marked the first proper on-board meal service as we understand it. To mark this event, BR Travellers Fare organised a centenary special in 1979. *Topaz* was included in the special and is seen at York. It bears the original Dalziel Pullman coat of arms that lasted from the 1907 takeover until 1960.

Left: In 1967, H P Bulmer Ltd (Cider Makers), of Hereford bought a set of Pullman cars for use in an exhibition train. This was the celebrated Bulmer's Cider Train, which is seen in Bulmer's eye-catching livery at an open day at Tyseley on 17th May 1970. Pullman identification has always caused problems because of confusion between schedule numbers and the identity on the car. The schedule number was derived from a series of lists drawn up by the Pullman Car Co at various times from 1915 to 1960, but omitted some pre-schedule cars of the 1870s. First class cars displayed a name, but Third class cars showed a number on the side. In the early days, it was rare that schedule and running numbers co-incided. Given schedule No 219, but lettered as 'Car No 64', this vehicle was a type P Third class parlour car built by Midland Carriage & Wagon Co in 1928. After sale to Bulmers, it was used as a restaurant car in the cider train, and known as *Christine*. It was sold to VSOE in 1986, and then resold, appearing on the Bluebell Railway.

Above: After a massive fleet refurbishment and expansion between 1921 and 1932, almost twenty years elapsed before any more Pullman cars were built, but the final flowering of the Pullman spirit came in 1960, when no fewer than 44 steel bodied cars were built by the Metropolitan-Cammell Carriage & Wagon Co. They were allocated schedule numbers 311 to 354, and in accordance with the usual tradition First class cars bore a name. Second class cars carried a number. For once this was the schedule number, instead of a separate running number (as with Car no 64 in the previous illustration). The cars were mounted on Mk I chassis, and carried a Mk I body structure, but with longer and shallower picture windows, and inward-opening doors. They appeared in the elegant Pullman livery of umber brown and cream with yellow lining, and carried the new "squashed" Pullman coat of arms. The roof was

white at first but weathered to grey. The whole batch went to the Eastern Region for the *Master Cutler,* the *Yorkshire Pullman, Tees-Tyne Pullman* and *Queen of Scots,* replacing the 1920s cars which were transferred to the Southern to replace even older stock. Pullman had been an independent company, but in 1954, BR obtained the ordinary shares, completing the process in 1962, after which Pullman was merged into overall BR operations. This was a tragic mistake, for BR had reached the nadir of its fortunes. For many years BR had been complacent, and needed re-organisation. Many hopelessly uneconomic lines still existed, and needed closure, but once closure is seen as progressive, rather than as a last resort, a negative mindset is introduced. By 1967, when Pullman operations were merged into the restaurant car departments of the BR regions, the First class cars were seen as too heavy for

their seating capacity with modern diesel traction. The answer was to reseat them to increase the capacity. This downgrading was accompanied by a change in livery. The handsome and distinctive Pullman colours were replaced by reversed BR corporate grey and blue, to produce an insipid livery. With the difference between Pullman firsts and Seconds eroded, there seemed little need for the Second class cars, and the kitchen Seconds were stored. Of the 44 cars built in 1960, the kitchen Seconds, Nos 332-346, were the most numerous class, and many of them came to Rugby where they could be stored in a reasonably safe environment away from vandals. Kitchen Second No 336 is seen at Rugby in November 1974. Six of these cars were later preserved, four of which ended up as static themed restaurants. No 336 was not preserved.

Right: Most of the Kitchen Seconds were still in Pullman colours when taken out of use, but a few did receive the reversed corporate colours. Car No 334 became E334E. The addition of an E suffix is strange as the cars had no pre-nationalisation background. One possible explanation is that it was to avoid confusion with the Mk I Diagram 17 Restaurant Firsts 306-342. In Pullman days, the depth of the cream band had been determined by the depth of the windows, to create a harmonious effect. With reversed colours, the standard depth of colour was applied. The traditional Pullman lettering above the windows disappeared, to be replace by an effete corporate image lower case Pullman branding applied in much the same way that Express Parcels or Newspaper inscriptions were added to parcels stock. The BR Design Panel, the authors of the depressing corporate image era, had a lot to answer for, not least for their impact upon the Pullman cars. E334E sits in the sidings next to the AEI works at Rugby in 1974. This site had once been the home of British Thompson Houston Co, then AEI, then GEC, now it is part of the French owned Alsthom group. As with 336, No 334 did not make it into preservation. The sight of these magnificent coaches lying out of use less than fifteen years after they were built was disheartening.

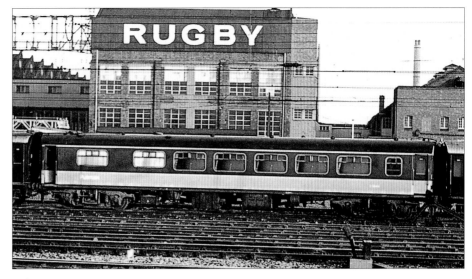

Centre right: The Kitchen Firsts, although downgraded in 1967-68, and re-liveried in reversed colours, continued to run on the Eastern Region. Thirteen of the Pullman Kitchen Firsts had been built to Diagram 130, making them the second most numerous type. They were numbered from 311 to 323, but in Pullman Company days bore names. The first of them, E311E, had been *Eagle*. The East Coast Pullman services continued to run until the introduction of the HST sets in 1978, but with the demise of the magnificent Pullman livery, much of the magic had gone long before they were displaced by the HSTs. We are looking at the kitchen side of E311E, identifiable because of its smaller opaque windows, at King's Cross station in July 1972.

Bottom right: As with many railway companies, Pullman re-used favourite names, and one of the 1960 cars, No 326, repeated the name of the legendary *Emerald* of 1910, which we have already encountered at Betws-y-Coed. The earlier car had given almost half a century of traffic service, and then some years as a camping coach. The new *Emerald* was to run in Pullman colours for just a few years, before being turned out in the reversed grey and blue livery. The arrival of the HSTs In 1978 spelled the end for Pullman services, and *Emerald* ran in the final *Yorkshire Pullman* on 5th May 1978. *Emerald* and *Eagle* were acquired for the NRM, both cars were restored to proper Pullman colours and included in the 'Travellers Fare' centenary special of 1979.

THE
**BOURNEMOUTH
BELLE**

Top and above: To conclude the Pullman section we will take a nostalgic look at the *Bournemouth Belle*. The LSWR had used Pullman drawing cars on some of its Waterloo to Bournemouth services from 1880, but it was the Southern Railway that introduced an all-Pullman train. The *Bournemouth Belle* commenced running on 5th July 1931 as a summer-only service but became all-year in January 1936. Discontinued during the Second World War, it resumed in 1946, but fell victim

to the electrification of the Bournemouth line, its demise coming on 9th July 1967. No 35028 *Clan Line* was one of my favourite 'Merchant Navy' class Pacifics. She is seen at Bournemouth Central station just prior to departure with the Up Belle at 16.37 hours. The train departed from Southampton at 17.15 and reached Waterloo at 18.53. The *Bournemouth Belle* was my favourite Pullman, and the only one I ever travelled on. It was a memorable birthday treat from my parents not long before the service

ended. The brochure, part of whose cover is reproduced above, was a souvenir of that trip. The Waterloo to Bournemouth fare was £2.4s (£2.20) first class and £1. 9s.3d second class with an 8s or 6s Pullman supplement. Luxury travel for the whole family cost less than an ordinary fare for one person today.

ROLLING STOCK SELECTION FOR THE MODELLER

For the modeller, there have always been difficulties in getting the correct mix of coaching stock on a layout. Availability of suitable stock was a problem facing the early enthusiasts. In pre-war days, the Leeds Model Company made lithographed paper sides that could be applied to standard wooden bodies. They included attractive LMS, LNER, GWR and Southern stock, but the lithos for LNER Gresley corridor stock were fitted to the same wooden bodies as LMS or SR carriages, regardless of length or even roof profile. From the 1920s to the 1950s, Hornby even produced four-wheel main line corridor stock. Edward Exley Ltd, the foremost manufacturer of coaches, produced attractive LMS dining cars and sleeping cars. The only problem was that they were the same length as standard stock and carried on four

Below: To celebrate Queen Victoria's Diamond Jubilee (1837-1897), the GWR decided to construct a new royal train. Five new carriages were built, each with the overhung roof design, whilst the royal Saloon itself was a rebuild, at the Queen's request, of the old GWR royal Saloon. The train included two full brakes, Nos 1069 and 1070, built under Lot 838 to Diagram K12. Fitted with special 10ft wheelbase bogies, both Brakes were eventually transferred to the Hotels and Refreshment Department. Repainted in 'brown stock' livery. They were used to carry stores to company hotels and refreshment rooms. No 1070, still in GWR livery, is on such duties at Leamington Spa in 1951. To the best of my knowledge, this and a similar view taken on the same occasion, are the only known colour photos of any stock from the 1897 GWR royal train in service.

wheel bogies, rather than 65 to 69 foot long 12 wheelers. The modeller had to do the best he could with what was available. Today we have a wide range of superb ready-to-run vehicles in 4mm scale, and a surprising selection of 4mm and 7mm kits. Other scales are also catered for, but not to the same extent, and there is no longer a need to accept an LMS, LNER, GWR or Southern coach produced from the same mould and lettered to suit. In the past, the best that the modeller could hope for was to create a plausible rake of stock, even though the individual vehicles might not be accurate representations of any specific prototype.

Today one can be more selective, and with that possibility has come a demand for much greater information. Once again, the modeller of today is better placed than in the past. In the 1960s, apart from a few drawings and articles in the model railway press, there was little information available on coaching stock, and virtually nothing on the formation of trains. The situation is quite different today with superb histories of the coaching stock of most of the major companies. The problem facing the modeller is not so much a shortage of data, but threading his way through the mass of data that does exist in order to find what he wants and will be satisfied with. By using a broad brush in this volume, my hope is that the modeller will see the aspects he wants to concentrate on, and how they fit in to the overall picture.

What kind of stock should the modeller operate? Period and location are the determining factors. Although BR Mk Is ran over most of the former LNWR system in the 1950s and 1960s, a rake of BR Mk Is would not be ideal on a period LNWR layout. Similarly, GWR Dean clerestories would not be appropriate for a Highland Railway layout. The predominant stock will depend on the period and the line, company or region, but throughout the steam age, there were plenty of interlopers to be found. As a child in the fifties and sixties, I enjoyed watching trains on the ex- LNWR/LMS line through Rugby, as there was a frequent service, and plenty to see, but the

nearby GC line was another favourite. Rugby is not associated with GWR 'Counties' or 'Halls', but through services operated from the Western and Southern Regions over the GC, and apart from engines, Western and Southern Region coaching stock appeared. The Southern rakes were particularly welcome as the only other opportunity to see green stock was on holidays in the south. In selecting stock for a layout, the modeller can achieve considerable diversity if this is kept in mind. On some lines the mix of stock could be breathtaking, classic examples including the legendary Somerset & Dorset, or the Midland & Great Northern. On summer Saturdays, an endless succession of specials took crowds to seaside resorts, and once again the variety of stock was legion. Inter-regional services proliferated in early BR days, and stock was cascaded from region to region or boundaries were redrawn. For example, when the former GCR's London Extension was handed to the LM Region, LNER stock was replaced by LM carriages, including LMS and BR Mk I stock, and LNER engines were replaced by 'Black Fives'. A transition layout could include Eastern Region Gresley or Thompson stock in maroon, LM Region Stanier and Ivatt stock, BR Mk Is, Southern Region equipment, and even early DMUs.

What sort of stock should you run on your layout? First of all, it should be suitable for the line you model. The average GWR branch line did not see GWR Dreadnought stock, Sleeping cars or a TPO. An auto coach or a two or three coach non-corridor set would be normal. Services might well be strengthened at peak periods by additional stock, or by through carriages. Milk traffic was common on many lines. Until the 1930s, this would be taken by churn to the station and loaded into ventilated vans. Thereafter the milk tank became more common, but this required a collecting point and a large catchment area if it was to be economic. Fishing ports might well see fish vans or even complete trains of such vehicles. Holiday resorts might have a sparse service in winter, but see a profusion of excursions on

summer Saturdays. This was a common pattern in the West of England, but was to be found elsewhere. Perhaps the extreme example of this was on the GNR(I) branch from Goraghwood to Warrenpoint. A succession of packed holiday specials would bring crowds from Belfast on a Summer weekend, but in winter, some services were operated by one of the road buses that the GNR(I) converted to run on rails.

Regular workings were based on sets that were laid down in the train marshalling books (see Appendix C). Specials were more varied, and were often comprised of stock retained for the summer peak traffic. This often included elderly vehicles. Such stock might come out of the carriage sidings for eight or ten Saturdays each year, and might well include many vehicles close to withdrawal, and which had not been repainted into the newest liveries. Such was the pressure of traffic at Bank Holiday weekends, that rakes of non-corridor suburban stock might be pressed into service, to the discomfort of many passengers, no doubt! Although the railway was running to capacity at such times, the operating officers still had to be careful about the selection of stock. If a 65-foot coach had clearance problems on weekdays, it would not clear during a Bank Holiday.

Throughout railway history, there have been individual lines with severe restrictions. The 'Hastings' DEMUs were built because of a tunnel of restricted bore. The Great Western built bogie stock that was no more than 11ft 3ins high for the Burry Port & Gwendraeth Valley line in South Wales. Gresley built

corridor stock in two lengths, providing short coaches for the Great Eastern section. The Caledonian railway even built some four-wheelers for the Balerno branch in Edinburgh as late as 1921. They had modern high domed elliptical roofs, and except for their length looked just like any contemporary stock. The 'Big Four' companies and BR produced Route Restriction books that detailed various prohibitions. In general, most main lines and many branches could take 57-foot stock, and many could take 62 or 63 foot stock. Longer vehicles such as the 65 and 70-foot diners and sleepers of the LNWR or LMS, and the GWR 70-foot Dreadnought stock, were restricted to particular routes on their home system. Apart from these general restrictions, there were specific restrictions for locations where clearances were exceptionally tight for one reason or another. This could be a narrow tunnel, a sharply curved platform that would foul a carriage as it overhung on the curve, or insufficient clearance if routed over a specific crossover. To give one example, 69-foot LMS sleeping cars could not work over the connections between platforms 8 and 10 at Preston.

Rolling stock restriction lists ran to many pages, and operating officers had to be familiar with these when selecting stock for regular or special trains. It would be impossible here to cover all the restrictions of even one of the 'Big Four', let alone the whole of BR. For those interested in further research on this topic, the restrictions were circulated in special booklets,

and were also to be found in the general or sectional appendices of the various companies and of BR. Copies of these can be found on second hand and antiquarian railway booksellers stalls at exhibitions and are an important source of data on many aspects of railway operation. The modeller who is planning a layout should certainly buy a suitable general/sectional appendix, as it will provide a mass of data, but the principles outlined in this section should give a good idea of the 'do's and don'ts'.

Below: A Stanier 'Black Five', No 44847 takes water at the up tank at the south end of Rugby Central station on 16th August 1966. The train, a typical four coach rake of Mk Is, is the 9.30am express to London Marylebone. In reality, semi-fast would be a better description, as such trains would call at quite moderate sized stations. Although we have illustrated a comparable service elsewhere in this book, it is important to emphasise that Pullman car trains, sleeping car services, restaurant cars and similar exotic vehicles were the exception, not the rule. Before the onset of dieselisation, of the DMU, and of Beeching, four to six coach sets of Mk1s or older pre nationalisation designs were common on express services on the secondary main lines from the south coast to the north of Scotland. For most modellers recreating the 1950 to the 1970s, a good rule of thumb is, take four Mk Is, and add other ingredients as desired. This is what it was like. This is what gives credibility to your layout.

STANDARD CODES FOR COACHING STOCK

Today we live in a world of e-mails, faxes and telephones and instant communication is easy. Vast amounts of data are routinely transmitted over the internet in seconds, but when information had to be written by hand or sent by telegraph, any method that saved time and effort was worthwhile. As the electric telegraph developed alongside the new railways, railwaymen started to use abbreviations in wiring data to one another. As different individuals would interpret abbreviations in different ways, a standard code was desirable. The bigger companies developed their own codes, some of which have entered into the enthusiast lexicon.

Some of the best known codes came from the Great Western Railway, and Siphon, Damo, Mica or Toad are familiar words to any Great Western devotee. I wonder how many GWR enthusiasts could say what a VON, a CON or a BON were ? Many years ago I was fortunate enough to discover a GWR Telegraph Department Carriage Stock report form from the 1870s. It provided condensed telegraph codes for Passenger Brakes, First, Second and Third class carriages, Composites, Slip Coaches, Horse Boxes, Open and Closed Carriage Trucks and even side lamps, roof lamps, tail lamps and connections. Each category had 'total on hand', 'wanted' and 'spare codes'. However, the GWR was still a mixed gauge railway, and officers needed to know whether stock ran on Brunel's seven-foot broad gauge or the Stephenson narrow gauge, as the GWR disdainfully called the interloper! Taking the codes, a First class broad gauge carriage on hand was FO; if a first class carriage was wanted it became FW and if spare FS. To distinguish the inferior narrow gauge stock from the real Great Western vehicles, narrow gauge coaches had an N suffix. A narrow gauge First on hand was an FON. Vans, Seconds and Composites were V, S, and C, but Third class coaches retained the old 'Parliamentary' designation, so were P. So thorough was the code, that it even included provision for broad gauge or narrow gauge tail lamps! The GWR 1870s list is the earliest rolling stock reporting code I have seen, and is reproduced as Fig 1

GREAT WESTERN RAILWAY.

TELEGRAPH DEPARTMENT.

_____ Station, July 8 __ 187

(2000) **CARRIAGE STOCK REPORT.**

C. R.   Code Time_____ No. of words_____ * The Number of figures only to be counted.

Station from _____   _Station to_ _____

W TERLOW & SONS LIMITED, Printers London Wall, London.

CLASS OF STOCK.		Broad Gauge.		Narrow Gauge.	
		CODE SIGNAL.	NUMBER.	CODE SIGNAL.	NUMBER.
Passenger Break Vans—					
Total No. on Hand	... ...	V O	...	V O N	...
Wanted Additional	... ...	V W	...	V W N	...
To Spare	... ...	V S	...	V S N	...
1st Class—					
Total No. on Hand	... ...	F O	—	F O N	...
Wanted Additional	... ...	F W	...	F W N	...
To Spare	... ...	F S	—	F S N	...
Composite—					
Total No. on Hand	... ...	C O	...	C O N	...
Wanted Additional	... ...	C W	...	C W N	...
To Spare	... ...	C S	...	C S N	—
2nd Class—					
Total No. on Hand	... ...	S O	—	S O N	—
Wanted Additional	... ...	S W	...	S W N	...
To Spare	... ...	S S	...	S S N	...
3rd Class—					
Total No. on Hand	... ...	P O	—	P O N	—
Wanted Additional	... ...	P W	...	P W N	...
To Spare	... ...	P S	...	P S N	...
Slip Coaches—					
Total No. on Hand	... ...	N O	...	N O N	...
Wanted Additional	... ...	N W	...	N W N	...
To Spare	... ...	N S	...	N S N	—
Horse Boxes—					
On Hand	... ...	H O	...	H O N	...
Wanted Additional	... ...	H W	...	H W N	...
To Spare	... ...	H S	...	H S N	...
Carriage Trucks—					
On Hand	... ...	A O	...	A O N	...
Wanted Additional	... ...	A W	...	A W N	...
To Spare	... ...	A S	—	A S N	—
Cov'd Carriage Trucks—					
Total No. on Hand	... ...	B O	...	B O N	...
Wanted Additional	... ...	B W	...	B W N	...
To Spare	... ...	B S	...	B S N	—
Side Lamps—					
Total No. on Hand	... ...	L O	...	L O N	...
Wanted Additional	... ...	L W	...	L W N	...
To Spare	... ...	L S	...	L S N	...
Roof Lamps—					
Total No. on Hand	... ...	R O	...	R O N	...
Wanted Additional	... ...	R W	...	R W N	...
To Spare	... ...	R S	...	R S N	—
Tail Lamps—					
Total No. on Hand	... ...	J O	...	J O N	...
Wanted Additional	... ...	J W	...	J W N	...
To Spare	... ...	J S	...	J S N	...
Connections—					
Total No. on Hand	... ...	X O	...	...	...
Wanted Additional	... ...	X W	...	...	...
To Spare	... ...	X S	...	...	...

Name of Station received | Receiving Clerk's | Station sent to | Time | Transmitting

LMS COACHING STOCK CODES

The 'Big Four' developed their own codes between 1923 and 1948. It would be impracticable to include all codes and modifications, but as the codes are a convenient and precise way to describe stock, they merit coverage. The first list is the LMS code list, to which I have added the 1950 BR codes for ease of cross-reference.

LMS Coaching Stock Codes

Type	LMS code	BR code
First Kitchen/Dining Car	1st RKC	RF
Composite	Compo RKC	RC
Third	Third RKC	RT
Unclassified	Common RKC	RU
Kitchen Buffet Car	BRC	RKB
Kitchen Only Car	KC	RK
First Class Vestibule Diner	QL (Dining)	RFO
Composite Vestibule Diner	VC (Dining)	RCO
Third Class Vestibule Diner	QF (Dining)	RTO
First Class Sleeping Car	SC	SLF
Composite Sleeping Car	CSC	SLC
Third Class Sleeping Car	SCT	SLT
Vestibule (i.e. Open) First	QL	FO
Vestibule Composite	VC	CO
Vestibule Third	QF	TO
Vestibule Third Brake	VH	BTO
Corridor/Vestibule First	CQL	semi-FO
Corridor First	CL	FK
Corridor Brake	E	BFK
Corridor Composite	CBC	CK
Corridor Composite Brake	CBB	BCK
Corridor Third	CF	TK
Corridor Third Brake	CH	BTK

Type	LMS code	BR code
Non Corridor First	L	F
Non Corridor First/Lavatory	LM	FL
Non Corridor Composite	BC	C
Non Corridor Composite/Lav	L&C	CL
Non Corridor Third	F	T
Non Corridor Third Brake	H	BT
Non Corridor Third Brake Lav	LH	BTL
Pass Brake with Gangway	CBR	BG
6w Brake with gangway	CR	BGZ
6w brake No gangway	R	BZ
Post Office Sorting Van	POR	POS
Post Office Stowage Van	PPR	POT

BR TELEGRAPH CODES FOR COACHING STOCK, 1950

Some of the LMS codes were easy to guess, such as SC for sleeping car, but many defy logical analysis. Other companies adopted different codes, so there was a risk of confusion, and one of the fruits of nationalisation was the new standard codes, which were based on the LNER practice, which came into force on 1st September 1950. This was an 88-page handbook entitled, *Standardisation of Railway Telegraph Message Codes*. Appendix A lists the 'STANDARD CODES FOR COACHING ROLLING STOCK'. The new codes were simple to use once the basic principles were grasped. These included F, S, T or C, for First, Second, Third and Composite. R for Restaurant, S for Sleeper, O for Open, K for 'Korridor' and B for Brake. The only reference in the codebook to 'gangway' was in the notes at the end of the section. This stated, 'the codes for corridor stock generally indicate that 'Gangway vehicles' are concerned.' Although corridor stock theoretically means gangwayed vehicles with a side corridor, in practice the term corridor stock was often applied to any vehicle with a corridor connection. In the codebook, the term 'Non Corridor Stock' was used rather than 'Non-Gangwayed'. By 1950, four-wheel and six-wheel stock was no longer used in passenger service, but a reminder of this could be seen in the addition of a Y suffix for a four-wheel Passenger Brake (BY), or a Z suffix for a six-wheel Brake (BZ).

68

APPENDIX "A"
STANDARD CODES FOR COACHING ROLLING STOCK

Type	Description	Code
PASSENGER VEHICLES		
Restaurant Kitchen Cars	First	RF
	Composite	RC
	Either Class	RU
	Third	RT
	Triplet	RTS
	Pantry Third	RTP
	Buffet Car	RB
	Kitchen Only	RK
Sleeping Cars	First Class	SLF
	First Class (Twin)	Twin SLF
	Composite	SLC
	Composite (Twin)	Twin SLC
	Third Class	SLT
Saloons	First Class	SF
	Third Class	ST
	Invalid Saloon	SI
Open Stock	First Class	FO
	Composite	CO
	Third Class	TO
	Third Class Brake	BTO
	Semi-Open First	Semi FO
	Second Class	SO
	Tourist Stock (Bucket Seats) Third Open	TTO
	Tourist Stock (Bucket Seats) Brake Third Open	TBTO
Corridor Stock	First Class	FK
	First Class Brake	BFK
	Second Class	SK
	Composite	CK
	Composite Brake	BCK
	Third Class	TK
	Third Class Brake	BTK

The 1950 codebook contained many other phrases relating to passenger traffic. A few examples may be of interest

AXIS Reserve following accommodation

PULSEAT Reserve seat/s ......class Pullman on ...... for .... Tickets will be issued here and supplementary fees collected.

JUG Reserve third class accommodation for prison party consisting of .... prisoner/s and escort.

SLEBO Reserve first class sleeping berth

THIRBO Reserve third class sleeping berth

CUTTLE Unable to reserve accommodation as requested

FAKIR Wire number of passengers expected

FLIGHT Weather unfavourable for liberation of pigeons received from your station. Instruct

FIRSIN First class single fare

FARO Third class single fare

CORBEX Can you provide train of third class corridor stock for ....

OPNEX Can you provide train of open thirds for following excursion (state if kitchen required)

SLOE Instruct driver and guards of undermentioned train to stop instead of slipping vehicles

SLIPPER Vehicles can now be slipped as booked

SLIGO The following train will stop instead of slipping at your station.

SILK Here without funds. Can you call at undermentioned address and collect fare, plus expenses as follows. Wire result at once.

EMCAR Special empty carriages

TRICARS Special train of empty cars on trial run.

NONCLERE Clerestory roofed vehicles must not be used

PASBAG ...... train conveying passengers and baggage for ..... as follows.

Some of the codes, if read by someone without access to the codebook, had potential for merriment or offence, such as Ape, Baboon, Prune, Rodent, Scab, Skunk or Slattern to mention just a few. One can imagine an exchange of messages between offices, SKUNK going one way, and SLATTERN coming back. However the exchange would have been entirely proper, as the first message says, 'Secure connection with...'. The reply means 'Cannot agree to your proposal'.

In 1956, the European Railways Union abolished three separate classes of travel in Europe, so BR was free to abandon the three class system on the continental boat trains. With this impediment out of the way, Third class was redesignated Second class from 3rd June 1956. Overnight many of the coach codes now became obsolete. and T (Third) codes were changed to S (Second). An RTO was now a RSO. A revised codebook was later issued.

Standard Codes for Coaching Rolling Stock (Continued)

Type	Description	Code
PASSENGER VEHICLES—*continued*		
Non-Corridor Stock (Bogies)	First Class	F
	First Class (Lavatory) ...	FL
	First Class Brake ...	BF
	First Class Brake (Lavatory)	BFL
	Composite	C
	Composite (Lavatory) ...	CL
	Composite Brake ...	BC
	Composite Brake (Lavatory)	BCL
	Third Class	T
	Third Class (Lavatory) ...	TL
	Third Class Brake ...	BT
	Third Class Brake (Lavatory)	BTL
Articulated Stock.—Should be indicated by the word "Twin," "Triple," "Quad," or "Quint" according to the number of vehicles in the set, the number of the set being shown when necessary and the letters ART.		
POST OFFICE VEHICLES		
	Post Office Sorting Van ...	POS
	Post Office Tender ...	POT
PASSENGER VANS		
Brake Vans	4-wheeled	BY
	6-wheeled (without gangways)	BZ
	6-wheeled (with gangways)	BGZ
	Bogie (without gangways)	B
	Bogie (with gangways) ...	BG
	Pigeon Van (Braked) ...	BP
	Milk Van (Braked) ...	BM

Standard Codes for Coaching Rolling Stock (Continued)

Type	Description	Code
MISCELLANEOUS TRAFFIC VANS		
	Parcels and Motor Van ...	PMV
	Horse Box	HB
	Special Cattle Van ...	SCV
	Open Carriage Truck ...	CTO
	Covered Carriage Truck	CCT

NOTES.

1. Variations in type or size of vehicles should be specified, e.g.—

    CTO Bogie CCT 21 ft. CCT 6 ft. wheelbase

2. The Codes for corridor stock generally indicate that "Gangway vehicles" are concerned. On occasions where it is necessary to specify a particular type of gangway the following codes should be used :—

    PG—Pullman Gangway.
    BS —British Standard Gangway.
    A —British Standard Gangway and Pullman Adaptors.

BR TELEGRAPH CODES FOR COACHING STOCK, JULY 1958

Apart from the substitution of S for T codes, new types of stock had appeared, such as the Kitchen Buffet car, RKB, or the restaurant/cafeteria car RCAF. Diesel codes have also appeared, and these have been shown as written and with a later update, these various lists give the modeller codes from 1930s through to the introduction of TOPS. A few terms merit comment

NC   Non-Corridor
ICS   Inter-Corridor Set (BSK, CK, BSK)
IDZ   Inter District Set (BS, C, BS)

Buckeye couplings and Pullman type gangways offered much greater resistance to telescoping in the event of an accident than the screw link coupling and the British Standard gangway. BR adopted the Pullman gangway for its Mk I stock. Without adaptors, this could not be connected to stock with British Standard gangways, and this had serious marshalling implications. In the marshalling books, several new codes appeared

Z   BR Standard Stock fitted with 'Buckeye' automatic couplers and Pullman gangways.
Y   Stock fitted with gangway adaptors
A   Class A stock

The official explanation that A meant Class A stock was of little help. Another instruction noted that the letter A was stencilled on the ends of the vehicles. Class A stock was fitted with British Standard gangways, so could be connected to itself, but not to Z stock, without the use of a Y adaptor fitted coach. In the marshalling circulars, Z and A stock often appear on the same train, but there is always a Y adaptor coach between them, so a train could consist of Z, Y, A, A, A, Y, Z, Y, A.

I had long been aware of the two main types of gangway, the British Standard and Pullman standard, but it was only after I unravelled the mysteries of A, Y and Z stock, that missing bits of the jigsaw dropped into place. It is an indication of how much more complicated the everyday world of the real railway is, than the picture we see from a distance as enthusiasts.

Railwaymen needed that level of precision, and just like the block telegraph codes used by signalmen, but which were meaningless to the outsider, they conveyed certainty that ordinary conversation could not match. The telegraph codes for coaching stock were a precise and economical instrument for railwaymen, but in the more detached atmosphere of railway enthusiasm, we may forget that railwaymen possessed a rich sense of humour. Many telegraphic names were amusing, and I sometimes wonder if the choice of names such as Toad, Mink or Goliath was by accident or whether it was someone with a delightful sense of humour. A story I was told by a retired GWR

APPENDIX "A"
STANDARD CODES FOR COACHING ROLLING STOCK

Type	Description	Code
PASSENGER VEHICLES		
Restaurant Cars	First, Open (loose chairs)	RFO
	Second, Open (loose chairs)	RSO
Restaurant Kitchen Cars	First	RF
	Composite	RC
	Either Class	RU
	Second	RS
	Triplet	RTS
	Pantry Second	RSP
	Buffet Car	RB
	Kitchen Only	RK
	Cafeteria Car	CAF
	Kitchen/Buffet Car	RKB
	Restaurant/Cafeteria Car	RCAF
	Miniature Buffet Car	RMB
Sleeping Cars	First	SLF
	First (Twin)	Twin SLF
	Composite	SLC
	Composite (Twin)	Twin SLC
	Second (non-pantry)	SLS
	Second (pantry)	SLSP
	Second two-berth (non-pantry)	SLST
	Second two-berth (pantry)	SLSTP
	Composite (two berth berths)	SLCT
Saloons	First	SF
	Second	SS
	Invalid Saloon	SI
Open Stock	First	FO
	Composite	CO
	Second Brake	BSO
	Semi-Open First	Semi FO
	Second	SO
	Tourist Stock (Bucket Seats) Second Open	TSO
	Tourist Stock (Bucket Seats) Brake Second Open	TBSO

71

Standard Codes for Coaching Rolling Stock   (Continued)

Type	Description	Code
PASSENGER VEHICLES—continued		
Corridor Stock	First	FK
	First Brake	BFK
	Second	SK
	Composite	CK
	Composite Brake	BCK
	Second Brake	BSK
Non-Corridor Stock (Bogies)	First	F
	First (Lavatory)	FL
	First Brake	BF
	First Brake (Lavatory)	BFL
	Composite	C
	Composite (Lavatory)	CL
	Composite Brake	BC
	Composite Brake (Lavatory)	BCL
	Second	S
	Second (Lavatory)	SL
	Second Brake	BS
	Second Brake (Lavatory)	BSL
Diesel Multiple Units	Motor First	MF
	Motor Compo Open	MC
	Motor Second Open	MS
	Motor Second Brake	MBS
	Motor Compo (Lavatory)	MCL
	Driving Trailer Compo (Lavatory)	DCL
	Driving Trailer Second (Lavatory)	DSL
	Trailer Second	TS
	Trailer Second Brake (Lavatory)	TBSL
	Trailer Second (Lavatory)	TSL
	Trailer Buffet First	TRBF
	Motor Trailer Second	MTS

Articulated Stock.—Should be indicated by the word "Twin", "Triple", "Quad", or "Quint" according to the number of vehicles in the set, the number of the set being shown when necessary and the letters ART.

employee is on a par with some of the classic railway tales. It deserves to be true, but alas I cannot vouch for it. As its author has gone to the Greater Swindon in the Sky to which all good GWR men undoubtedly go, I cannot question him further, but after the 'heavy going' of the codes, it strikes a welcome relief.

In Victorian and Edwardian Britain, travelling theatrical companies gave performances at local theatres, and on a Saturday night after the last performance, the troupe with all their costumes, props and scenery, would hurry to the station where passenger stock and scenery trucks would be waiting. Early scenery trucks had been coded Pythons, Goliaths and Scorpions, but theatrical impresarios believed that bigger was better. The GWR obliged with some 50 foot bogie vans in 1911. Side doors and end doors were provided, and the vans were accorded the telegraph code Monster, no doubt on account of their size. This much of the story can be confirmed.

It is said that a GWR employee was speaking in the pub with another employee he had not seen for some time, and the subject of Monsters turned up. Neither man was confused as they knew what a Monster was. A newspaper reporter overheard this, but not being versed in the GWR telegraph codes, interpreted it differently. Being a good reporter, he sought further details, and learned of a sea creature that rivalled the Loch Ness monster. The story was replete with many convincing details, not least the fact that the Monster frequented a remote part of the coastline only accessible by a long walk from the nearest GWR station. This was only natural, for no self-respecting monster would cavort in full view of the public off Brighton beach or Blackpool sands. Many local people had seen the monster, but had been cautioned against talking, lest it create panic. The reporter was only being let in on the secret as he had overheard.

The reporter, on the track of a sensational scoop, hurried to his editor, who dispatched him to the haunts of the monster. The police resolutely denied the story, which given the news blackout, was strong evidence for the monster theory. Most local people discounted it, but a few admitted they had seen curious things. The reporter being a diligent man, or enjoying the beautiful to which he had been sent, all expenses paid, searched for the monster, but tiring of his pursuit, or, perhaps more likely, his editor tiring of his expense account, called off the search.

The reporter returned home, no wiser but perhaps not very much sadder as he had had a good holiday, and chanced to meet his informant in the pub, whereupon he recounted his woes. His informant, being a tactful man, forbore from admitting him to the ranks of men versed in the lore of Great Western telegraph codes. The story, or even a watered down version of it, deserves to be true. It blends humour with real life.

Standard Codes for Coaching Rolling Stock (Continued)

Type	Description	Code
PASSENGER VEHICLES—*continued*		
Corridor Stock	First	FK
	First Brake	BFK

71 *Delete* all matter relating to Diesel Multiple Units and insert :—

	Description	Code
Diesel Stock	Motor First	MF
	Motor Second	MS
	Motor Compo	MC
	Motor Brake First	MBF
	Motor Brake Second	MBS
	Motor Brake Compo	MBC
	Motor Brake Second Lavatory	MBSL
	Motor First Lavatory	MFL
	Motor Second Lavatory	MSL
	Motor Compo Lavatory	MCL
	Driving Trailer First	DTF
	Driving Trailer Second	DTS
	Driving Trailer Compo	DTC
	Driving Trailer First Lavatory	DTFL
	Driving Trailer Second Lavatory	DTSL
	Driving Trailer Compo Lavatory	DTCL
	Trailer First	TF
	Trailer Second	TS
	Trailer Compo	TC
	Trailer First Buffet	TFRB
	Trailer Second Buffet	TSRB
	Trailer Compo Buffet	TCRB
	Trailer First Lavatory	TFL
	Trailer Second Lavatory	TSL
	Trailer Compo Lavatory	TCL
	Trailer Brake First Lavatory	TBFL
	Trailer Brake Second Lavatory	TBSL
	Trailer Brake Compo Lavatory	TBCL
	Motor Parcels and Miscellaneous Van	MPMV
	Diesel Rail Bus	DRB

72

Standard Codes for Coaching Rolling Stock (Continued)

Type	Description	Code
POST OFFICE VEHICLES		
	Post Office Sorting Van ...	POS
	Post Office Tender ...	POT
PASSENGER VANS		
Brake Vans	4-wheeled	BY
	6-wheeled (without gangways)	BZ
	6-wheeled (with gangways)	BGZ
	Bogie (without gangways)	B
	Bogie (with gangways) ...	BG
	Pigeon Van (Braked) ...	BP
	Milk Van (Braked) ...	BM
MISCELLANEOUS TRAFFIC VANS		
	Parcels and Miscellaneous Van	PMV
	Horse Box	HB
	Special Cattle Van ...	SCV
	Open Carriage Truck ...	CTO
	Covered Carriage Truck	CCT

Authorised *Tiered* **NOTES** (*or Van* TCV)

1. Variations in type or size of vehicles should be specified, e.g.—
   CTO Bogie   CCT 21 ft.   CCT 6 ft. wheelbase.

2. The Codes for corridor stock generally indicate that "Gangway vehicles" are concerned. On occasions where it is necessary to specify a particular type of gangway the following codes should be used:—
   PG—Pullman Gangway.
   BSG—British Standard Gangway.
   A—British Standard Gangway and Pullman Adaptors.

E.R.O. 19120/4

London Midland and Scottish Railway Company.
(WESTERN DIVISION.)

PASSENGER TRAIN
MARSHALLING ARRANGEMENTS
From MAY 2nd, 1932, until further notice.

PASSENGER TRAINS MUST BE MADE UP STRICTLY IN ACCORDANCE WITH THE ARRANGEMENTS SHOWN HEREIN, AND MUST NOT BE ALTERED WITHOUT AUTHORITY FROM THE DIVISIONAL SUPERINTENDENT OF OPERATION.

THE LOADING OF TRAINS MUST BE CLOSELY WATCHED AND ANY DAILY SHORTAGE OF ROOM, OR LIGHT LOADING, IMMEDIATELY REPORTED.

Where Brake Carriages are shown in this Marshalling Book next to the engine, they must, as far as practicable, be run with the Brake compartment in front. When changing this type of vehicle owing to stoppage for repairs or other causes, Marshalling Inspectors, Foremen, and Shunters must see that the vehicle to be substituted has the Brake compartment at the leading end, taking steps to have it turned, if necessary.

TONNAGE LOADING.

No Train must be made up to more than 500 tons, and not more than 15 Bogie Vehicles may be run on any Train, except where laid down herein, or specially authorised by the Divisional Superintendent of Operation.

EXPLANATION OF REFERENCES.

§	Steel Vehicles.	†	Four or Six Wheeled Stock.
‡	Empty Trains.	N.C.	Non Corridor.
M.	Mondays excepted.	M.O.	Mondays only.
M.S.	Mondays and Saturdays excepted.	M.S.O.	Mondays and Saturdays only, &c.

CREWE, *April 23rd*, 1932.   **CHIEF GENERAL SUPERINTENDENT.**

McCorquodale & Co., Ltd., London.

PASSENGER TRAIN MARSHALLING ARRANGEMENTS

As I have emphasised, passenger trains were not made up at random from whatever vehicles happened to be in the carriage sidings. Formations were carefully planned by the operating officers to allow for the potential traffic, to conform with the capabilities of the locomotives hauling the train and any restrictions imposed by the route to be taken.

Train formations were set out in the Passenger Train Marshalling Instructions. The cover of the booklet which included the instructions for the Western Division of the LMS, commencing on 2nd May 1932, is reproduced on the page opposite. Unlike timetables or the general/sectional appendices, relatively few examples of these books, seem to have survived.

The 1932 arrangements book describes the formation of between four and seven trains per page, depending on their complexity. The LMS still gave a full description in the marshalling circular, rather than codes. Page 13, reproduced here, covers four services from Carlisle, two of which started from Glasgow and one from Aberdeen.

The journey north of the border would appear in the LMS Northern Division marshalling book. The 12.13pm Carlisle to Euston consists of two portions, a seven coach set from Glasgow and a four-coach set from Edinburgh. The Glasgow section has a Kitchen car which is flanked by Vestibule (Open) coaches where meals would be served. The Edinburgh portion comprises a Third Brake, a Third Restaurant car, a First Corridor Vestibule (a mixed Corridor/Open vehicle) and a Composite Brake. The inclusion of a Restaurant car in the four-coach Edinburgh portion shows that catering vehicles can run on short trains.

The 12.28pm Carlisle to Birmingham is a complex working with a mail van from Glasgow to Southampton, a GWR Composite Brake through coach from Glasgow to Plymouth, a Crewe section, a Birmingham section, and Edinburgh-Birmingham and Edinburgh-Crewe portions. It consists of six sections in all, and is remarshalled Crewe, with the Southampton mail van going on to a Manchester-Bristol service and the GWR through coach being attached to a GWR service. In a 12 coach train, the largest portion is of five carriages, and as one would expect, there are no fewer than six Brakes.

The 12.41pm Carlisle to Euston is another complex working, with portions from Perth, Dundee and Aberdeen. At Preston, more stock is added, including passenger sections from Whitehaven and Barrow and a milk tank. The train gains more vehicles at Stafford and sheds its milk tank at Rugby. The 1.00pm ex Carlisle includes a, 'narrow corridor set', used because of restricted tunnel clearances on the West Cumberland section of the LMS. In Appendix 2,

I referred to through coaches and interlopers from afar. Here is factual data that an LMS modeller who sets his layout against the dramatic backdrop of Shap or Beattock can include a GWR Composite Brake in his roster.

The use of through coaches was an aspect of the British Railway scene from mid-Victorian times to the end of the steam age in the 1960s. Trains combined and split in a way that the modern railwayman would find astonishing, for the companies felt that through workings promoted their image, encouraged traffic, and benefited the passenger. Perhaps the extreme example of this was the Aberdeen-Penzance through service. This commenced in 1921 as a joint venture between the GCR, NER, NBR, and GWR, and used existing trains for much of the 785-mile journey. The through coaches were initially North British or Great Western, giving the extraordinary prospect of an NBR composite trundling along the sea wall at Dawlish and crossing the Saltash viaduct, and the equally unlikely thought of the chocolate and cream colours of the GWR crossing the Firth and the Tay. However unlikely it seems, a GWR modeller could run an NBR coach on his layout, or vice versa. Provided we do not stretch credulity too far, as modellers we can gain from this rich past, adding through coaches to meet our own particular wishes.

13

Marshalling.	Balance.	Marshalling.	Balance.
12.13 p.m., CARLISLE TO EUSTON.		**12.41 p.m., CARLISLE TO EUSTON.**	
(10.0 a.m. from Glasgow.)		(6.45 a.m. from Aberdeen.)	
(10.0 a.m. from Edinburgh.)		(8.20 a.m. from Dundee.)	
		(9.0 a.m. from Perth.)	
§Third Brake ⎫		Brake Van ⎫	**B**
Third ⎪		Compo. Restaurant ⎬ Perth Euston	**A**
Third Vestibule (60 ft.) ⎪		Car (65 ft.) ⎭	
Third Vestibule (60 ft.) ⎬ Glasgow	10 0 a.m.	Compo. Brake (60 ft.)—Dundee Euston	10 0 a.m.
Kitchen Car ⎪ Euston	11Su30a.m.	Composite ⎱ Aberdeen	10 0 a.m.
First Corr. Vestibule ⎪		§Third Brake ⎰ Euston	
First Brake ⎭		Attach rear Preston :—	
§Third Brake ⎫		aFirst Brake ⎱ Whitehaven	
Third Restaurant Car ⎬ Edinburgh	10 0 a.m.	aThird ⎰ Euston	
First Corr. Vestibule ⎪ Euston	11Su30a.m.	aThird (SO) —Barrow Euston	
Compo. Brake ⎭		c†Milk Tank ⎱ Carlisle Bow	
		cBrake Van ⎰	
Tonnage—345.		Attach front Stafford (behind Perth Euston Van) :—	
		bBrake Van (Mails)(ThO) ⎱ Manchester	
		bCompo. Brake ⎬ (L. Rd.) Euston	
12.28 p.m., CARLISLE TO BIRMINGHAM.		bThird (FO) ⎰	
(10.7 a.m. from Glasgow.)		**a** Received off 11.20 a.m. from Whitehaven.	
(10.0 a.m. from Edinburgh.)		**b** Received off 2.40 p.m. from Manchester.	
cBrake Van (TFO) ⎱ Glasgow		**c** Received off 9.50 a.m. from Carlisle. Transferred Rugby to 5.45 p.m. to Willesden.	
(Mails) ⎰ Southampton		**A** 1.11 p.m. from Crewe.	
aG.W. Compo. Brake ⎱ Glasgow	8 45 a.m.	**B** Received off 10.15 p.m. from Birmingham.	
⎰ Plymouth			
Composite ⎱ Glasgow	9 31 a.m.	Tonnage—158 Carlisle.	
Third Brake ⎬ Crewe		251 (S), 279 (SO) Preston.	
Compo. Restaurant ⎪		280 (MTWO), 308 (ThFSO) Stafford.	
Car (65 ft.) ⎭	**B**	242 (MTWO), 270 (ThFSO) Rugby.	
Third Vestibule(60 ft.) ⎱ Glasgow			
CThird (FSO) ⎰ Birmingham	—		
Compo. Brake (60 ft.) ⎱	11 45 a.m.	**1.0 p.m., CARLISLE TO LANCASTER**	
Third Vestibule ⎪		**(via Whitehaven).**	
Compo. Brake (60 ft.) ⎬ Edinburgh	11 45 a.m.	aNarrow Corridor Set ⎱ Bradford	CD
CThird (FSO) ⎪ Birmingham	—	(4 vehicles) ⎰	
Third Brake (TFO) —Edinburgh Crewe	**A**	Attach front Maryport :—	
		bCompo. Brake —Euston	A
Attach front Crewe :—		bThird Brake ⎱	CD
Third (FSO) —Birmingham		bComposite ⎬ Manchester (Ex.)	
a Transferred Crewe to 3.5 p.m., Manchester to Bristol.		BbBrake Van ⎰	B
		Attach rear Barrow :—	
c Transferred Crewe to 5.5 p.m. to G.W. Line.		aCompo. Restaurant ⎱ Leeds	10 35 a.m.
		Car (65 ft.) ⎰	
A Balanced 3.50 a.m. parcels (WO), 2.55 p.m. (Sun), Crewe to Glasgow.		**a** Transferred Carnforth to 4.57 p.m. to Leeds.	
		b Transferred Lancaster to 4.5 p.m., Windermere to Manchester (Ex.).	
B Works 11.45 a.m., Birmingham to Crewe. 2.9 p.m., Crewe to Preston, 4.12 p.m., Preston to Glasgow.		**A** 10.35 a.m., Euston to Whitehaven, 12.0 noon, Whitehaven to Maryport.	
		B Commences June 2nd ; balanced 9.40 a.m. from Manchester (Vic.).	
C Commence June 3rd.			
		Tonnage—110 Carlisle.	
Tonnage—243 (TF), 296 (TFO) Carlisle.		195 Maryport ⎱	
159 (FS), 187 (FSO) Crewe.		237 Barrow ⎬ Until June 1st.	
		84 Carnforth ⎰	
56 tons extra throughout (FSO), commencing June 3rd.		220 Maryport ⎱	
		262 Barrow ⎬ From June 2nd.	
		110 Carnforth ⎰	

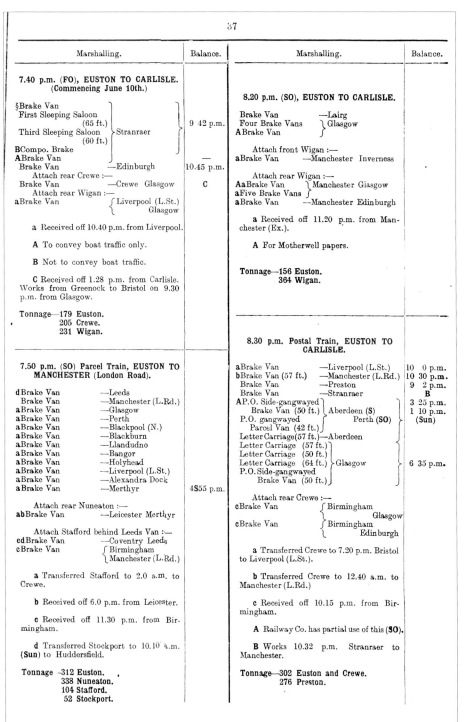

		37		
Marshalling.		**Balance.**	**Marshalling.**	**Balance.**

7.40 p.m. (FO), EUSTON TO CARLISLE.
(Commencing June 10th.)

§Brake Van ⎫
First Sleeping Saloon (65 ft.) ⎪
Third Sleeping Saloon (60 ft.) ⎬ Stranraer — 9 42 p.m.
BCompo. Brake ⎪
ABrake Van ⎭

Brake Van —Edinburgh — 10.45 p.m.

Attach rear Crewe :—
Brake Van —Crewe Glasgow — C

Attach rear Wigan :—
aBrake Van ⎰ Liverpool (L.St.)
⎱ Glasgow

a Received off 10.40 p.m. from Liverpool.

A To convey boat traffic only.

B Not to convey boat traffic.

C Received off 1.28 p.m. from Carlisle. Works from Greenock to Bristol on 9.30 p.m. from Glasgow.

Tonnage—179 Euston.
205 Crewe.
231 Wigan.

7.50 p.m. (SO) Parcel Train, EUSTON TO MANCHESTER (London Road).

dBrake Van —Leeds
Brake Van —Manchester (L.Rd.)
aBrake Van —Glasgow
aBrake Van —Perth
aBrake Van —Blackpool (N.)
aBrake Van —Blackburn
aBrake Van —Llandudno
aBrake Van —Bangor
aBrake Van —Holyhead
aBrake Van —Liverpool (L.St.)
aBrake Van —Alexandra Dock
aBrake Van —Merthyr — 4S55 p.m.

Attach rear Nuneaton :—
abBrake Van —Leicester Merthyr

Attach Stafford behind Leeds Van :—
cdBrake Van —Coventry Leeds
cBrake Van ⎰ Birmingham
⎱ Manchester (L.Rd.)

a Transferred Stafford to 2.0 a.m. to Crewe.

b Received off 6.0 p.m. from Leicester.

c Received off 11.30 p.m. from Birmingham.

d Transferred Stockport to 10.10 a.m. (Sun) to Huddersfield.

Tonnage –312 Euston.
338 Nuneaton.
104 Stafford.
52 Stockport.

8.20 p.m. (SO), EUSTON TO CARLISLE.

Brake Van —Lairg
Four Brake Vans ⎱ Glasgow
ABrake Van ⎰

Attach front Wigan :—
aBrake Van —Manchester Inverness

Attach rear Wigan :—
AaBrake Van ⎱ Manchester Glasgow
aFive Brake Vans ⎰
aBrake Van —Manchester Edinburgh

a Received off 11.20 p.m. from Manchester (Ex.).

A For Motherwell papers.

Tonnage—156 Euston.
364 Wigan.

8.30 p.m. Postal Train, EUSTON TO CARLISLE.

aBrake Van —Liverpool (L.St.) — 10 0 p.m.
bBrake Van (57 ft.) —Manchester (L.Rd.) — 10 30 p.m.
Brake Van —Preston — 9 2 p.m.
Brake Van —Stranraer — B
A P.O. Side-gangwayed ⎱ — 3 25 p.m.
Brake Van (50 ft.) ⎱ Aberdeen (S)
P.O. gangwayed ⎬ Perth (SO) — 1 10 p.m.
Parcel Van (42 ft.) ⎰ (Sun)
Letter Carriage(57 ft.)—Aberdeen
Letter Carriage (57 ft.) ⎱
Letter Carriage (50 ft.) ⎬
Letter Carriage (64 ft.) ⎬ Glasgow — 6 35 p.m.
P.O. Side-gangwayed ⎰
Brake Van (50 ft.) ⎰

Attach rear Crewe :—
cBrake Van ⎰ Birmingham
⎱ Glasgow
cBrake Van ⎰ Birmingham
⎱ Edinburgh

a Transferred Crewe to 7.20 p.m. Bristol to Liverpool (L.St.).

b Transferred Crewe to 12.40 a.m. to Manchester (L.Rd.).

c Received off 10.15 p.m. from Birmingham.

A Railway Co. has partial use of this (SO).

B Works 10.32 p.m. Stranraer to Manchester.

Tonnage—302 Euston and Crewe.
276 Preston.

Above: Page 37 of the marshalling circular for 1932 covers the sleeping car and parcels services leaving Euston between 7.40pm and 8.30pm. The 7.40pm Euston to Carlisle (Fridays Only) leaves Euston with six carriages, five for Stranraer, where connection will be made with the boat to Larne, and a Full Brake for Edinburgh. Additional vans are added at Crewe and Wigan, increasing the tare from 179 to 231 tons. In this eight-coach train, the passenger accommodation comprises a First Sleeper, a Third Sleeper and just one day carriage, a Composite Brake. The 7.50pm (SO) Euston to Manchester leaves London with a dozen Brakes for a dozen different destinations. It picks up an extra van at Nuneaton, increasing the train load to 338 tons, but sheds eleven Brakes at Stafford. Two of the original BGs go on, together with a pair of BGs from Coventry and Birmingham. The train is shunted again at Stockport, two vans going to Leeds, and one Euston van and one van from Birmingham arrive in Manchester. The 8.20pm Euston-Carlisle is another newspaper and parcels train that gains extra portions front and rear at Wigan. Finally, we come to one of the most celebrated trains of all, the 8.30pm Down Postal from Euston to Carlisle. This conveys side-gangwayed postal stock including an ex-LNWR 42 foot postal car. There are portions for Liverpool, Manchester, Preston, Stranraer, Aberdeen, Glasgow, and Edinburgh.

The Marshalling circulars laid down the normal train formation. In today's computerised and highly regulated railway, if there is a sudden rush of passengers the train gets overcrowded, or they do not travel. The system is not geared up to add extra stock at a moment's notice, nor does the stock exist to do so. The LMS had a more accommodating attitude. The LMS instructions to staff covered the situation.

'Extra Vehicles must not be attached to passenger trains for the conveyance of passengers, unless authorised in the programme, or other special train notices, or by the Divisional Train Passenger Control Office, or the District Goods and Passenger Manager.

In exceptional circumstances, when there is insufficient time to telephone the Divisional Passenger Train Control, or District Goods and Passenger Manager, Swansea, as the case may be, the Station Master may attach additional vehicles for the accommodation of passengers, provided the maximum tonnage for the class of engine working the train is not exceeded, and the working of it is not likely to be otherwise upset en route.

Advice must at once be given by telephone to the Divisional Passenger Train Controller, District Goods and Passenger Manager, Swansea, or the District Controller (in cases where he is responsible for the supervision of the working of the train) stating precisely what has been done.

The Divisional Passenger Train Control, or District Goods and Passenger Manager, Swansea, must be advised immediately it is known horse boxes, wagons of cattle, fish traffic, etc., for conveyance by passenger train are likely to pass.'

This rule was typical of the LMS approach to management. A high proportion of senior LMS officers had risen through the ranks. They had first hand experience at the sharp end of the business and were well aware that there was not always time or opportunity to contact headquarters. Many of them had faced such situations in their younger days, and had used common sense as their guide.

In any organisation there will be good and poor staff, and that would include Station Masters, but Divisional Managers expected that a Station Master at an important station would have sufficient experience and intelligence to act responsibly. If he acted foolishly in overloading trains regularly, or did nothing, then it called into doubt his suitability for the post, or for further advancement.

By giving responsible officers that freedom, the company not only allowed the man at the sharp end to use his judgment for the benefit of the passengers, but also had an excellent way of assessing the calibre of its men. It may be that the government departments and businesses of today could benefit from a study of the management techniques of the LMS and the other great railway companies of the past.

The next two pages come from the LM Region (Western Division) passenger train marshalling circular commencing 16th September 1957. Instead of a printed book, it is duplicated, and clarity suffers. From July 1956, third class had been redesignated Second, so the reference is to Second class stock rather than third class.

Page 7, right, lists four early evening workings from Birmingham. The 6.00pm (FSX) to Liverpool Lime St comprises eleven carriages when it leaves Birmingham, the first five vehicles being Mk I stock. Somewhat confusingly, the marshalling circular saves space by abbreviations such as 2CK., for a pair of CKs. The next vehicle is a category Y SK, or in other words a Corridor Second with gangway adaptors. These six carriages form the Lime St portion of the train. The next five vehicles have an A in the left hand column, so are older LMS stock with British standard gangways. They are detached at Crewe and go on to Manchester.

On Fridays the train runs as two separate workings, a Manchester portion leaving at 6.00pm, and the Liverpool portion departing at 6.10pm. The Liverpool set of 5 Mk Is and an adaptor coach is strengthened by four SKs and one BSK, all class A stock.

The 7.40pm Birmingham to Euston is class A stock throughout. The passenger portion consists of two four-coach passenger sets, both consisting of the following vehicles; BSK, CK, SK, BSK. They will be split at Euston and return north on separate services. Three BGs are attached at the rear of the train, two of which have come from Sutton Park, where there was a large parcels office. The train will run from Rugby via the Northampton Loop, picking up a BG at Northampton for Euston, and a Q (as required) working, of up to three four-wheeled 'Vanfits' as well. One of these is destined for Southampton, and will be detached at Bletchley to make connection with the 4.55am parcels train to Oxford. It will then work forward to Didcot probably over the Didcot, Newbury and Southampton line

Page 15, reproduced on page 90, lists some remarkable workings, commencing with the 7.20pm Chester to Crewe. On weekdays, the leading set is a three-coach non-corridor IDZ, or Inter-District Set, consisting of a Brake Second, a Composite and another Brake Second. Next comes a BG from Birkenhead to Birmingham, and a four coach corridor set similar to the previous train, viz. BSK, CK, SK, BSK. On Saturdays, the non-corridor IDZ set is replaced by another BSK, CK, SK, BSK set, and an additional SK is added at the rear of the train. At Crewe the train will split, the rear portion going on the Birmingham.

The 9.25pm Chester to Llandudno is equally instructive. Out of seven vehicles (on weekdays) three are BSKs and one is a BG, giving no more than 198 seats in a 213 ton train. Once again, the basis of the train is a four coach BSK, SK, CK, BSK formation which operates between Crewe, Chester and Llandudno. This is strengthened by a BG and two passenger carriages that have been detached from the 5.35pm Euston to Holyhead express. Such through workings were a feature of the steam age.

Marshalling	Balance	Marshalling	Balance
6.0pm (FSX) 6.5pm (SO) BIRMINGHAM TO LIVERPOOL (Lime St.)		**7.40pm BIRMINGHAM TO EUSTON (Class "A" Stock)**	
Z BSK (24))		BSK (24))))	
Z SK (48)) Liverpool)	11.40am	CK (18/24))))	
Z 2CK (24/18)) (L.St.))		SK (42)))	B
Z BSK (24))		BSK (24))) Euston)	
Y SK (42))		BSK (24))))	
Aa SK (42))	12.40pm	CK (18/24))))	C
Aa BSK (24))) Manchester)		SK (42))))	
Aa SK (42))) (L.Rd.))	B	BSK (24))))	
Aa CK (18/24))))		BG (SX)	
Aa BSK (24))))		a BG)Sutton Park	
		a BG (SX) "Q")Euston	
a. Transferred Crewe to 7.44pm (FSX) 7.53pm (SO) Crewe to Manchester.		**Attach rear Northampton :-** BG (SX) - Euston	
B. 3.48am (FX) from Crewe. Work 12.40pm (MSX), 3.55pm (Sun) Manchester to Euston.		b Vanfit (SX) "Q" - Nuneaton Euston	
		b Vanfit (SX) "Q" - Atherstone Euston	
BIRMINGHAM - 11/354 CREWE - 6/199		bc Vanfit (SX) "Q" - Atherstone Southampton	
6.0pm (FO) BIRMINGHAM TO MANCHESTER (London Rd.)		a. Received off 5.45pm Pcls. from Sutton Park.	
A SK* (42)))	12.40pm	b. Received off 5.33pm from Rugby.	
A BSK (24)))		c. Transferred Bletchley to 4.55am Pcls. to Oxford.	
A SK (42)))	B	B. 12. Onn from Euston. Work 4.15pm (MSX) Euston to Bletchley, 6.40am (TO) Euston to Windermere, 2.25am (Sun) Euston to Northampton.	
A CK (18/24))) Manchester)		C. 7.55am from Rugby. Work 11.56pm (SX) Euston to Bletchley, 8.50am (Sun) Euston to Northampton.	
A BSK (24))) (L.Rd.))			
CK (18/24)))	Div1/R.		
4SK (42)))	Crewe.		
BSK (24)))			
Attach rear Crewe :- BG - Stockport		BIRMINGHAM - 10/298 (SX) 9/273 (SO)	
B. 3.48am (FO) from Crewe. Work 7.50am (SO) Manchester to Crewe.		NORTHAMPTON - 11/323 (SX) 9/273 (SO) (excluding "Q" Vans).	
BIRMINGHAM - 11/341 CREWE - 12/366 STOCKPORT - 11/341			
6.10pm (FO) BIRMINGHAM TO LIVERPOOL (Lime St.)			
Z BSK (24)))			
Z SK (48)))			
Z 2CK (24/18)))			
Z BSK (24)) Liverpool)	11.40am		
Y SK (42)) (L.St.))			
A 4SK (42)))	Div1/R.		
A BSK (24)))	Crewe.		
11/354			

The 8.00am and 11.50am Colne to Stockport give further examples of through coach working. Colne is a medium sized town lying on the Midland/LYR route from Skipton to Burnley. It is not on any of the main trunk routes, but to take one example, the 11.50am provides a convenient connection to London. The train comprises a Y adaptor BSK, and a pair of A corridor coaches, a CK and an SK. At Stockport, it will be attached to the rear of the 2.00pm Manchester-Euston express. Most of the stock for the Manchester-Euston train is Mk I, including the rear BSK when the train leaves Manchester (London Rd), so the adaptor BSK is needed to connect the two portions together.

The 12.02am (Mondays only) Crewe to York is another unusual working. Loading to eight coaches, the train includes a couple of SKs, a POS (Post Office Sorting carriage) a BCK, SK, BSK set and a BG. The POS has come in off a Sunday evening working from Cardiff, whilst the BG has arrived from Shrewsbury.

I have covered train marshalling and through coach working in some depth, as correct marshalling of passenger services is a complex and little appreciated art. I first learned something of it in the Isle of Man and the Isle of Wight, where there was no corridor stock, but heavy traffic and small engines required careful selection of stock to maximise carrying capacity on peak services. The canvas was small but that made it easier to understand the basic needs. Standing beside any main line, express trains thundered by one after the other, and even if one paid attention to the coaching stock, and few enthusiasts did, there was no time to appreciate why the train was made up in any particular way. These pages give some of the answers. Although the rest of the train is class A stock, the leading coach on the 11.50am Colne to Stockport must have gangway adaptors, as it will be attached to a Mk I at the rear of the Manchester-Euston express. If the set were the other way round, the corridor connections could not be coupled up. This is a detailed point, and few modellers will want to worry about British standard or Pullman corridor connections, but the formation of some of the other services reveals their past or future, for example the use of two BSK, CK, SK, BSK rakes on a train which has combined or will split.

The modeller can create a train with two or more portions, using his own common sense and the trains listed in this section, as a guide. Some principles stand out. Few long distance trains were without adequate Brake or First class accommodation. If there was just ONE coach in a portion, it was usually a BCK. If there were two coaches, a CK-BSK combination was usual. Three coach sets usually consisted of a BSK-CK-BSK formation, but the 12.02am Crewe to York consisted of a BCK-SK-BSK, which is another way of achieving the same result. Four coach sets often consisted of a BSK-CK-SK-BSK.

In the 1932 marshalling book, there is a catering car on a four-coach set. A full Kitchen car offered no seating capacity, and even a Restaurant or Buffet car only provided limited accommodation, so a Restaurant car would invariably work with one or more Open carriages. Using later terminology the 1932 train comprised a BTK, RT, semi-FO and BCK. With only four coaches, two of which included brake sections, and one a kitchen section, the proportion of third class seating is surprisingly low, but third class passengers could be accommodated in the BTK, the RT and in the third class compartments in the BCK.

As we go beyond four coach rakes, more Thirds or Composites are needed, or the train can be made up of two or more portions. Trains serving a prestigious area may have more first class accommodation. For example, many Manchester businessmen lived in Southport, so the expresses leaving Manchester about 5.00pm for Southport contained a high proportion of first class stock, and even included a Club car before the war. This was a First Class Saloon. Travel was conditional on a first class rail ticket, and approval by the regular travellers on the club car.

On non-corridor services, similar principles apply. With few exceptions, trains offered first class accommodation as well as Second or Third. In two coach formations a BT-C set was common. With three-coach sets, BT-C-BT was normal, (which is the basis of the BR IDZ set). However we have illustrated a three-coach set on the GW & GC Joint with just one Brake vehicle. This offers higher seating capacity in a given train length, so is well suited to suburban workings. Lavatory stock was used on medium length runs, but would not be diagrammed for short distance services in a busy commuter area.

Realistic parcels stock operation offers many challenges to the modeller. The 7.50pm (SO) Euston to Manchester is instructive, as it leaves

Marshalling	Balance	Marshalling	Balance
7.20pm CHESTER TO CREWE		**8. 0am COLNE TO STOCKPORT**	
IDZ (24/216) (SX)	-	BSK (24))	1SX19pm
A BSK (24) (SO)	B	CK (18/24)) Stockport	130 40pm
A CK (18/24) (SO)) Crewe		Za CK (24/18))	
A SK (42) (SO))		Ya BSK (24))	B
A BSK (24) (SO))		Aa BSK (24)))	
		Aa CK (18/24))) Euston	C
ab BG Birkenhead Birmingham		Aa SK (42)))	
		Aa BSK (24)))	
aA BSK (24)))			
aA CK (18/24)))		a. Transferred Stockport to 10. 0am Manchester to Euston.	
aA SK (42)) Birmingham)	C	B. 9.45am from Euston. Work 2.30pm (SX) Euston to Southport 9.45am (MO) Euston to Colne.	
aA BSK (24)))		C. 2.45pm from Euston Work 2.45pm (MX) Euston to Colne, 11.50pm (Sun) Euston to Stafford.	
a SK (42) (SO))	D		
		8/251.	
a. Transferred Crewe to 7. 5pm Liverpool to Birmingham.			
b. Received off 5.54pm from Birkenhead.		**11. 50am COLNE TO STOCKPORT**	
B. 4.26pm (SO) from Crewe. Work 6. 0am (TO) Crewe to Warrington.		Ya BSK (24)))	6SX30pm
C. 5.54pm (SX) from Birkenhead, 4.26pm (SO) from Crewe. Work 9.50am (MSX) Birmingham to Stoke, 5.56am (SO) Birmingham to Stafford 12.20am (Sun) Birmingham to Euston.		Aa CK (18/24)) Euston)	3SO45pm
		Aa SK (42) (FO))	
		a. Transferred Stockport to 2. 0pm Manchester to Euston.	
D. Work 12.20am (Sun) Birmingham to Euston.		2/62 (FX), 3/93 (FO)	
8/234 (SX) 10/304 (SO)			
9.25pm CHESTER TO LLANDUDNO		**12. 2am (MO) CREWE TO YORK**	
Za CK (24/18)) Euston		2SK (42) - Leeds	
Ya BSK (24)) Llandudno		a POS) Shrewsbury	
a BG (SX))		) York	
A BSK (24)))		A BCK (12/21)))	
A SK (42)))		A SK (42)) York)	B
A CK (18/24))) Llandudno	B	A BSK (24)))	
A BSK (24)))		b BG - Shrewsbury York	
a. Received off 5.35pm (SX) from Euston 8.36pm (SO) from Crewe.		a. Received off 6.15pm (Sun) from Cardiff.	
B. 6. 8pm (SX) from Crewe, 4.40pm (SO) from Llandudno Work 8.10am (MSX) Llandudno to Llandudno Jn, 2.45pm (SO) Llandudno to Crewe 12.45pm (Sun) Llandudno to Chester.		b. Received off 5.55pm from Shrewsbury.	
		B. 12.10pm (Sun) from Shrewsbury. Work 9.50pm York to Swansea.	
7/213 (SX), 6/188 (SO).		8/240	

London with a dozen Brakes for a dozen different destinations. This train conveys even more portions than the legendary *Atlantic Coast Express,* albeit that it is only a parcels working. Suitable stock for parcels trains includes gangwayed Brake vans (four or six wheeled or bogies), Horse boxes, Prize Cattle vans, CCTs, Bogie Scenery trucks, Pigeon vans, PLVs, PMVs, Luggage & Parcels vans, Fish wagons, Milk tanks and more, depending on the period modelled and the type of traffic. However there are some pitfalls to catch the unwary. Horse boxes, Fish wagons, Bogie Scenery trucks and CCTs do not ordinarily have any guards accommodation, a brake wheel and valve and facilities for the guard. In steam days any coaching stock train had to include a vehicle from which the guard can apply the continuous brake. In creating parcels trains, the modeller can include Fish wagons, Scenery Trucks, CCTs and the rest, but he MUST include

at least one Brake vehicle in any set of stock that will run as a separate train.

To give some simple examples, the BR MK I utility van or CCT did not have a guard's brake valve or wheel, so a train of four CCTs is incorrect. The Mk I BG did have a guard's compartment, so add a BG, and you have a realistic train. If a CCT is detached at an intermediate station, that is fine, but if the BG is detached, there is no proper provision for the guard. The CCT can run on a passenger train, but the train must have a Brake vehicle, so a CK, FK, SK, CCT combination is incorrect. A BSK, FK, SK, CCT combination would be permissible. In creating realistic parcels trains, the modeller must make sure that there is at least one Brake vehicle in any train. The same applies with fish or milk trains. The guard did not sit on a fish box in a smelly van, or swim in a milk tanker. He travelled in a suitable van.

STONE'S ELECTRIC LIGHTING

The earliest carriages were unlit, or illuminated by feeble oil lamps. By the 1870s oil lamp design had improved considerably, but the next step forward was to use compressed gas carried in pressure cylinders below the chassis. The lighting was much superior to the oil lamp, but a number of accidents in which coaching stock caught fire as a result of rupture of the cylinders or pipe work, with the escaping gas being ignited by live coals from locomotive fireboxes, revealed the inherent dangers of gas lighting. Even so, a few gas lit coaches survived into BR days.

The nineteenth century was a period of amazing scientific and engineering progress. The electric telegraph had developed alongside the infant steam railway. The telephone transmitted human voice, electric dynamos enabled wealthy and far-sighted householders to illuminate their homes by electricity, and the lighting of coaching stock was not far behind. There were numerous problems to solve, and the leading exponent of electric carriage lighting in the British Isles was J Stone & Co of Deptford, London. Stone's Electric Light system was developed in the latter part of the nineteenth century.

There were several problems to overcome. Given the capacity of the lead-acid batteries of the day, it would be impossible to draw power from batteries slung beneath the coaches for a long journey, and recharging times at terminals would drastically reduce availability of stock. In theory it would be easy to connect a dynamo to one of the coach axles, so that the motion of the train turned the dynamo and powered the lamps. If only a dynamo were used, as soon as the train slowed down as it approached a station, the lights would dim and they would go out when it came to a stand. The answer was to combine a dynamo and battery, with an automatic charging system so that the dynamo lit the bulbs and charged the battery as the train travelled along. Victorian engineers had developed belt drives for workshop equipment to a high degree, so a simple belt drive presented no difficulties. Victorian engineers also knew how to vary speeds on belt drives so a large pulley wheel was fitted to one of the carriage axles, and a small pulley wheel to the dynamo itself, ensuring a high speed of rotation. However, the output of a dynamo depends on the speed of rotation. On a fast train, the dynamo could be rotated too fast, overloading the bulbs or batteries when they were charging. Therefore, the dynamo was not rigidly anchored to the frame, but suspended off-centre from a swing link L. The dynamo was so positioned that when the carriage was at rest, the dynamo was pulled out of the position in which it would naturally hang. The angle of the suspension link could be adjusted by means of a cross arm and adjusting screw (T and N). This permitted the electrician to adjust the tension

on the belt. When the train was in motion, the pull on the belt would be proportional to the speed, and if this exceeded the weight on the belt due to the one sided suspension of the dynamo, the dynamo would be pulled towards the driving pulley, reducing the tension on the belt, and enabling it to slip, regulating the speed and hence the power output to safe level.

A carriage must be able to run in both directions. In theory the guard could connect every dynamo for a given direction before the train started, but a moment of forgetfulness could wreck the batteries, and every time the train had to shunt, every dynamo would need to be switched. The answer was a governor, in which metal spheres fly out on hinged arms, and as the coach speeded up, a rocking arm was pushed along a shaft. This would not connect the dynamo to the batteries or the lamps until a 24-volt supply was being produced, but it additionally pressed a see-saw lever in the appropriate direction, depending on the direction of travel. In either case, current initially flowed to the carriage lighting, but as the power output increased, some power was diverted via the connections made by the see-saw arm to the batteries. In one direction, No 1 battery was charged. In the other direction No 2 battery was charged. The lights could be switched off, or run on half power or full power, by means of a simple switch. An automatic lubricating system was also provided. Stones' gave comprehensive instructions of installing their lighting system, and as there was a potential market in converting older stock, the system was devised to allow for this. Many modellers like to get obscure details correct on coaching stock, but I have sometimes seen excellent models where the dynamo has been hung the wrong way, because the information is not readily available to the modeller. Stones explained that the precise location of the dynamo would depend on the design of the frame, as it needed to be hung from a suitable frame member. The position was not critical as the length of the belt could be adjusted once the suspension link had been installed. Two battery boxes were normally mounted lengthways under the chassis. They were secured to the chassis by means of iron straps passing round the box and under it lengthways. Stones noted that an additional stay from the underframe to the bottom of the box was helpful in reducing strain as a result of shunting moves. The individual accumulators were fitted in the battery boxes, and were charged for 36 hours before first use.

With new coaches, the wiring was commonly run inside, but with older stock, this could be difficult and unsightly. Stones recommended running the three main cables along the top of the roof, there being two positive cables and one negative. A line was marked along the centre line of the roof, and holes drilled through the roof for the wires to each lamp. Then small wooden strips were nailed by means brass pins to the roof at approximately 9 inch centres, the centres of the blocks corresponding with the line marked on the roof. These blocks were to raise the cables so that water would not collect against them. A short flange Z was

screwed over each hole, the joint being made waterproof by red lead or putty. The three lead covered cables were laid down over the row of blocks. The insulation was broken at each light fitting, a branch wire soldered to the main cable and the joint insulated. Small iron domes or covers were then bedded in red lead or putty and screwed down on top of the terminal block. Usually the wires were stapled to the blocks by means of brass saddles, but if electric and oil lit stock were to work together, with lamp men walking from roof to roof to change oil lamps, Stones advocated a wood casing over the cables to avoid damage from the men's hobnail boots. Stones recommended that the cables should run down the inside of a partition, but if this was not possible, they could be run down one end of the coach. Either way, an on/off master switch was located outside at one end of the coach. The wiring was then taken along the underframe to the battery boxes and the dynamo.

This wiring system is sometimes seen as a distant item on pictures of Victorian and Edwardian stock. It is seldom that such photos give the detail we desire as modellers, and as Stone's installation manual is rarely found, and few modellers have been able to study the fittings on an externally wired coach, I have described it in some detail. Apart from reading the Stone's manual from which this description comes, my father used to have an adage, 'Don't guess, find out', so I ended up scrambling about on a coach roof almost thirty years ago. Although Stones recommended an independent installation per coach, they also provided fittings for slave coaches, where one accumulator coach provided power for a slave coach. In this instance, the roof cables were continued over the end of the roof in a graceful swan neck curve and when not in use rested in eye bolts screwed to the end of the carriage body. When a slave coach was to be connected, the cables were removed from the eyebolts and coupled by means of a jaw arrangement to the corresponding cables on the adjacent vehicle. Obviously, the two cables had to be sufficiently long to couple adjoining carriages together.

One further modification may be mentioned. Occasionally one encounters a coach with a dynamo, but apparently without batteries. Stone's recommended that the batteries be slung below the underframe, but they could be mounted above the frame in battery boxes in a brake compartment. In practice, this was not a good idea, as the inevitable leakage from the batteries did the chassis no good at all. I have studied such an installation, and its long-term consequences.

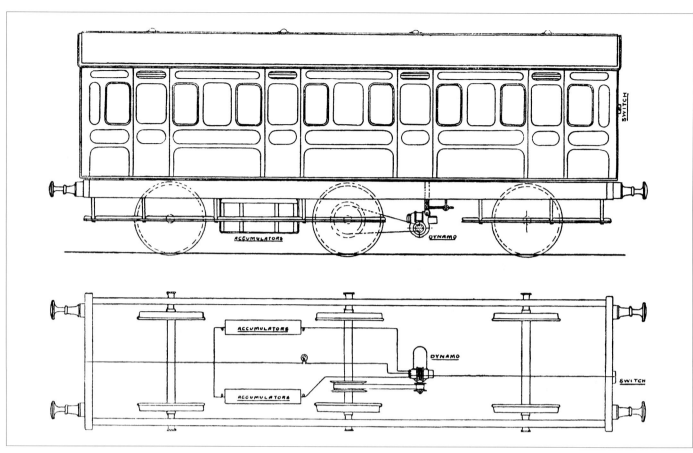

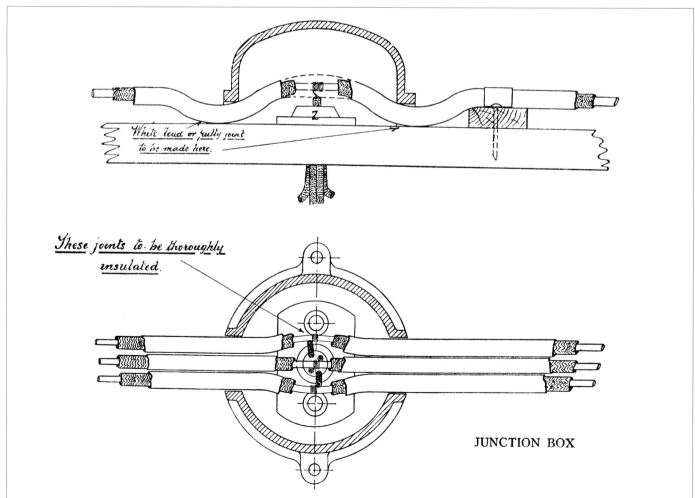

JUNCTION BOX

GLOSSARY

In preparing this Glossary, I have kept the descriptions as simple as possible, to help the readers to whom it should be the most use, namely those unfamiliar with coaching stock terminology. The changing face of railways means that many things that were common in my childhood are seldom to be seen today. I doubt if many readers will have seen a coupe compartment or a flitch plate, to give just two examples. Terms such as BCK (Brake Composite Corridor), FO (First Open) appear in the Coaching Stock Codes appendix on pages 81-85, so are not repeated here.

Anti Collision Fenders Saw-tooth device on the ends of coaches introduced by J G Robinson on GCR stock in 1915 to reduce risk of telescoping of stock in an accident. A modern version with a cone and socket has been developed by the Health & Safety Executive to be fitted to any Mk I stock in use after 1/01/2003. Drawbacks; can only work if adjacent vehicles are fitted.

Articulated stock System where two bogie coaches share one bogie. Can be a twin, ie two coaches with one articulation, triplet (3 coaches, with two articulations, quad (4) and quint (5)

Auto Coach A GWR term. Used on short distance services where steam locos would have to run round frequently. The coach has end windows and a driving compartment, and a remote control system so that the driver can control the regulator and brakes of the engine remotely. See also, motor train.

Battery boxes Large boxes usually below the solebar in which the batteries are located.

Battery electric stock A vehicle drawing power from batteries: It may be battery only, or battery/third rail electric (see page 72).

Beading Narrow strips of wood secured over panel joints on wooden bodied coaches to make joints weather proof, and for decoration. Often picked out in different colours. Could be half round or almost flat.

BG Short name for bogie brake van with gangway.

Bogie A truck, usually 4 wheeled, but sometimes 6-wheel, with a centre pivot, so that it is free to rotate.

Bogie coach A coach fitted with bogies permitting a longer vehicle than would be possible with a rigid wheelbase design. Also rides better.

Chassis The underframe or chassis comprises the longitudinal members, or solebars, the transverse members at the ends known as headstocks, the other inner frame members, tie bolts, tie rods, kingposts, trusses, etc.

Clerestory Roof A shallow curved roof with a central raised portion to give greater headroom, with small windows in the sides of the raised section giving better lighting. See pages 19, 21, 24 62, 65, 74, 79,

Compartment Early British stock was derived from stage coaches. The compartment was the full width of the coach with a door on each side flanked by small windows. Seats were fitted to the transverse partition walls. When corridor stock was introduced, the compartment was narrowed to permit a side corridor. American stock was usually 'open' i.e. a long saloon with few or no intermediate transverse partitions and a centre walkway or aisle. This is now standard on British stock.

Composite Chassis A chassis built partly of wood and partly of steel. See page 7.

Composite or Compo A coach with more than one class of accommodation, eg a '1/3 compo' had 1st and 3rd compartments, a tri-compo had 1st, 2nd and 3rd accommodation for passengers.

Corridor A side passage on one side of a coach giving access to the compartments via internal doors. The normal form of British long distance coach from the early 1900s to the 1950s. Now rare other than on sleeping cars.

Corridor Connections Also called gangways – connect corridors of adjoining coaches. There were two main types, the British standard and the Pullman gangway (which was used by the Pullman Car Company, LNER & BR Mk Is).

Coupe Compartment A 'half compartment', i.e. a seat against one partition, and legroom, but the other partition is without a seat. Used where there was not room for a full-sized compartment.

Couplings, Buckeye Couplings shaped rather like a fist which lock together to provide a very smooth ride, without the jolting associated with screw couplings or three link. Greater resistance to overriding in the event of an accident, and very strong.

Couplings, Screw Derived from the early hook and three-link coupling. The middle link is replaced by a threaded shaft with a handle. The outer link is put over the hook of the adjoining coach, and the screw tightened up to make the coupling rigid. Less jolting than with 3 link, but not as good as Buckeye.

Cove roof A compound curved roof used by the LNWR. Now obsolete

Diagram The page number in the official diagram books showing an outline drawing of the type of vehicle.

Diesel-Electric Multiple Unit DEMU, a Southern Region version of the DMU, but with electric transmission, rather than mechanical or hydraulic.

Diesel Multiple Unit A diesel powered railcar train consisting of a driving power car and powered or unpowered cars with a driving position at the other end of the set. Control circuits allow the driver to work all engines from the leading control position.

Doors, left or right hung From the 1860s onwards, carriage doors were normally 'left' hung. The hinges were on the left hand side of the door, and the handle to the right, as seen from the outside. In the early days of railways, right hung doors had been common. See the S&D coach on page 16 or GNSR coach on page 96.

Droplight The window in a coach door which can be lowered. See pages 16/17.

Dynamo. In effect, the opposite to an electric motor. With a motor you apply electric power and it rotates. With a dynamo you rotate it, and electricity is produced. The movement of the wheels when the train is moving is taken to the power pulley of the dynamo by a belt. See pages 7 and 91, 92).

Electric Multiple Unit An electrically powered railcar train consisting of a driving power car and powered or unpowered cars with a driving position at the other end of the set. Control circuits allow the driver to work all traction motors from the leading control position.

Elliptical roof A roof that is sharply curved at the edges and with a gentle curve in the centre. Permits good use of loading gauge profile. Can be low or high elliptical.

Externally framed body A timber passenger coach gained its strength from the vertical and horizontal frame members. Panelling was ordinarily applied outside the framework, though there would usually be an inside skin as well to reduce drafts, make for a neater finish, and give added strength. A few companies such as the Stockton & Darlington or the Highland used single skinned coaches with external framing, the body pillars being visible. See the S&D coach on page 16. The NLR coach above it is more typical.

Family Saloon In the days of big well-off families who travelled with maids and governesses, a family might charter a four or six-wheel saloon to attach to a passenger train for their private use. See page 17 for an example.

Flat roof An almost flat roof, though in fact with a very shallow curve.

Flitch Plates Iron or steel plates bolted to the outer face of a wooden solebar. See MNR coach on pages 18/19 for an example.

Gangway see corridor connections

Grab handle Fixed metal handle on the exterior of a coach near the doors.

Grained Finish Wood must be protected from moisture. Coaches could be painted or varnished. A special technique using a stiff 'scrumble' brush produced the elegant grained wood effect on many pre-group coaches. The last significant users were the LNER and GNR(I).

Headstocks Also called bufferbeams, the transverse chassis member at the end of a coach, to which the buffer and couplings are fitted.

Integral Construction In traditional rolling stock design, the chassis took all the structural load, and the body was merely bolted to it. In integral construction, they are built as one, and the body is load bearing. This permits a stronger vehicle for a lower tare weight.

Kingpost A vertical pillar below the solebar through which the truss rod passes.

Lavatory Stock	Although corridor coaches customarily have lavatories, the term was used for non-gangwayed vehicles with lavatories accessible to one or a few compartments in the vehicle.
Marshalling Circular	Also 'Marshalling Arrangements Book'. An internal use book giving the formation of trains. An important source document for modellers.
Matchboarded	Most wood bodied stock was built with panels, the joints being concealed by beading. A few companies built stock with narrow planking, usually applied vertically. This was called matchboarding. See GCR 'Barnum' coach page 22. For an unusual example see Page 46.
Motor Train	An alternative term for auto train. Often belled as 3-1-2
Non-Corridor	Technically this means stock without a side corridor, so an 'open' coach with a central aisle is not corridor stock, but in everyday usage, railwaymen used it for stock without corridor connections. The correct term for this would be non-gangwayed.
Non-Gangwayed	See above – this means stock without gangways connecting adjoining coaches.
Painting & Varnishing	Wooden bodied carriages were rubbed down, received coats of stopping and priming, being rubbed down between each coat. They received undercoats, a number of coats of body colour, and then several coats of varnish. Between general overhauls, they might be patch painted (and varnished) to deal with local damage, or re-varnished to protect the wood and freshen up the body paintwork.
Panelling	Wooden carriages were built on a wood framework of vertical and horizontal members clad with rectangular sheet of wood, or panels. The joints between panels were covered with strips pf wood called beading. Before welded construction became common, early steel-bodied coaches were built with steel panels in a similar fashion. These might or might not be beaded. Even if unbeaded, a painted beading effect might be applied.
Pigeon Van	A bogie van with shelving which was suitable to convey racing pigeons in wicker hampers from their home lofts to a release point.
Push-Pull	An alternative name for auto train or motor train. A very good name, as it emphasises that the engine pulls it train in one direction, but pushes it on the return journey.
Quad Art	Articulated set consisting of four-vehicles. Best known were the Gresley quad-art suburban sets (see page 27)
Quarterlight	The door window (or droplight) on many early stage coaches and railway coaches was flanked by quadrant shaped (or quarter circle) windows, the straight edges being next to the door and at the top. For this reason they were often called quarterlights, and the name stuck when rectangular windows were adopted instead.
Railbus	A small usually four-wheeled self propelled passenger carriage. The earliest examples were converted road buses, hence the name. See pages 50/57.
Railcar	A self propelled passenger carriage. (see pages 47 et seq). Can be steam, diesel or electrically powered. Most British diesel railcars could be connected in multiple with other units and controlled from one position, hence the term DMU. A railcar without multiple unit control is not technically a DMU, but a railcar.
Running Gear	Components allowing the coach to run, wheels, axleboxes, axlebox guides, axletrees or W irons on four-wheel and six-wheel stock, bogies on eight and 12 wheelers, brakes, brake rigging and vacuum cylinders. See pages 6-8.
Siphon	A railway telegraph code used by the GWR, and not related to the usual dictionary meaning. A ventilated van originally with slatted sides used for milk churns that had to be kept cool by a current of air as the train travelled. The GWR Siphon eventually became a louvred bogie van that was suited to virtually any urgent traffic. (see page 32)
Slip coach	To permit passengers to alight from express trains at less important stations, the last coach could be fitted with a special slip coupling which disengaged when the train was travelling at speed. The train continued at running speed, and the coach ran into the platform under its own momentum, a highly trained slip-guard slowing it to a stand by use of the coach brakes. The vacuum brake system had to be isolated when the coach slipped, otherwise the train and the slip coach would both make an emergency brake application. See page 25. The last slip working was in 1960.
Solebar	The outermost longitudinal members in a chassis or underframe. Originally of wood, latterly of steel. Integral construction stock has no separate frame members.
Tare	The weight of the vehicle when empty.
Telegraph Codes	To assist railway staff in describing stock, standard telegraph codes were developed. See pages 81-85. As the codes were short, for example a Brake Third Corridor was a BTK, they were used in everyday speech as well.
Telescoping	In an accident, one coach may override the next coach, pushing its way into the body in much the same was as a telescope is closed. This is the main cause of casualties in rail accidents. Buckeye couplers, Pullman gangways and high end resistance have been successfully used to minimise this danger.
Tierods	See truss rods
TOPS	Total Operations Processing System. A computerised stock location and identification system introduced by BR in 1972.
Travelling Post Office (or TPO)	A coach with letter sorting racks used by postal workers to sort mail en route to speed delivery. Until the 1970s, many TPOs had nets to pick up mail bags at speed and similar systems to unload mailbags, so avoiding the need for frequent stops to pick up/set down mail, see pages 15,29,31,43.
Truss rods.	Steel rods secured to the headstocks, and angled down between the bogies and held apart from the solebars by kingposts. This gives greater strength to the solebar.
Underframe	See chassis
Vacuum brakes	From the 1889 Act until late in the twentieth century, the main continuous brake in use on Britain's railways was the vacuum brake. The rival Westinghouse air brake was used by some companies, mostly in Scotland, and the east of England. Except on preserved lines, the vacuum brake has been phased out in favour of air brakes.
Ventilators	Before air conditioning, many different types existed. In Victorian days, sliding wooden shutters blocked off louvres above the droplights in the doors. See pages 6,16,18,20,21. On saloon stock, extra ventilators were provided above the saloon windows. Torpedo ventilators were fitted to the roof. They comprised a metal hoop with projecting cones and a rotating shutter inside the compartment. See pages 24,25 and 33. The 'shell' ventilator worked in the same way but instead of the cones, they looked like a seashell. Underground stock often had roof mounted air scoops, half pointing one way and half the other.

Top: To conclude this survey we will look at two classic vehicles, one dating from the dawn of the railway age, but the other from the golden age of railways, but which survived into modern times. The Great North of Scotland Railway was fifth in size of the independent Scottish railways in 1923. It served an area north and west of Aberdeen. Its best known route, now lifted for over thirty years, ran west from the Granite City to Ballater, which was convenient for Queen Victoria's Scottish retreat at Balmoral. This grounded GNSR 1850s four-wheeler was photographed at Cambus o'May station on the banks of the lovely River Dee on 5th July 1969. Brown Marshalls had supplied identical three compartment 18-seat First class carriages for the opening of the first section of the GNSR in 1854, and the design was in production until 1883. These vehicles, which were 21ft 9in over buffers, and weighed 9 tons, were typical of the period, and include many classic Victorian features such as semi flat beading, square panelling (except along the top of the window

line), and round-ended buffer beams. In contrast to many later designs, the doors are hinged or hung to the right, not to the left. The survival of such an early grounded body at this date is unusual, but may be explained by the frequency with which Royal trains traversed the line. Regular repainting had preserved the body in remarkable condition for over a century. Sadly, the closure of the Ballater route was to spell its demise.

Above: R E L Maunsell was born in Dublin in 1868, and trained under H A Ivatt, the locomotive superintendent of the Great Southern & Western Railway of Ireland, so he had first hand experience of Victorian railway life. After spells at Horwich and in India, he returned to the GS&WR as Chief Mechanical Engineer, before becoming Locomotive, Carriage & Wagon Superintendent of the SE&CR, and finally of the Southern Railway. He retired in 1937. He was an innovative and far sighted engineer, and realised the need for cost

effective equipment long before most of his contemporaries. One example was the fleet of planked Southern passenger vans which survived in large numbers until the early 1980s. Astonishingly, they all descended from a prototype van built at Ashford as long ago as 1919. Four-wheeled guards' vans, passenger luggage vans and utility vans were turned out by the hundred by the SR and British Railways, construction not ceasing until December 1955. SR PLV (passenger luggage van) No 2208 was built in January 1935, and transferred to departmental duties in 1959. In its new role with the Outdoor Machinery Section, it housed a Mobile Generator Set. This provided standby electricity in the event of a power failure stopping services on the Southern Region Waterloo & City underground line (otherwise known as 'the drain'). Stationed at Waterloo within yards of the rail lift that gave access to this line, DS70020 seldom moved away from Waterloo. A thirty-year departmental career ended in 1989.